DECENTRALISATION AND EMPOWERMENT OF DALIT WOMEN

DECENTRALISATION AND EMPOWERMENT OF DALIT WOMEN

Dr. Sundara Raj. T
Assistant Professor
Department of Sociology
Periyar Palkalai Nager
Periyar University
Salem- 636 011 (Tamil Nadu)
(India)

DPH

DISCOVERY PUBLISHING HOUSE PVT. LTD.
INDIA

Published by:
Namit Wasan
DISCOVERY PUBLISHING HOUSE PVT. LTD.
4383/4B, Ansari Road, Darya Ganj
New Delhi-110 002 (India)
Phone : +91-11-23279245, 43596064-65
Fax : +91-11-23253475
E-mail : discoverypublishinghouse@gmail.com
namitwasan9@gmail.com
sales@discoverypublishinggroup.com
web : www.discoverypublishinggroup.com

First Edition: **2018**

ISBN: 978-93-86841-46-9

Decentralisation and Empowerment of Dalit Women

Printed at:
Infinity Imaging Systems
Delhi

Foreword

Even though the constitution of India advocates equality for all, the deep rooted caste system has never allowed the lower caste people to be on par with others. Even after 70 years of freedom, not much has changed in terms of social mixing or relationship across caste barriers. Positioned at the bottom of India's caste, class and gender hierarchies, Dalit women experience more prevalent gender-and-caste discrimination as the result of unfair social, economic and political power equations. Their socio-economic status and lack of political voice, combined with the risk factors of being Dalit and female, increase their vulnerability. Violence against Dalit women, which is on the rise in India, is the core outcome of gender-based inequalities, shaped and intensified by the caste system. It presents a clear evidence of widespread exploitation and discrimination against these women who are often suppressed in terms of power in a patriarchal society and the unfair treatment against their communities based on caste. As the National Commission for Women has commented, "in the commission of offences against... Scheduled Caste [Dalit] Women the offenders try to establish their authority and humiliate the community by subjecting their women to indecent and inhuman treatment, including sexual assault, parading naked, using filthy language, etc."

Efforts has been taken, both by the government and NGOs to ensure personal security to Dalit women, through empowering the Dalit community and their women folks, making them aware of their rights and by making them strong enough to fight back the entrenched gender-and-caste biased notions of (in)equality and (in)justice. One such conscious attempt which was made to incorporate gender issues into this process of decentralisation planning is enactments of the 73rd and 74th Constitutional Amendments, which mandated 33 percent representation of women at all three levels of the PRIs. This forms an opportunity structure for SC women to come to the mainstream of the society. In order to understand, therefore, the reality of impact of development programmes on Dalit community and Dalit women in particular, this book has made an analysis of the democratic decentralisation in the state of Kerala and its impact on Dalit women. This analytical lens, grounded in Dalit women's subjective experiences, highlights the extent to which SC women are aware about the developmental opportunities as well as the choices made out by them in the process of development. This study also tries to analyse how far democratic decentralization has contributed to the Social, economic and political empowerment of SC women through the participation in various schemes. The vast body of literature presented through this book gives the reader an opportunity to critically explore the various models of empowerment through the different agencies of empowerment. The book is unique as it is speaks the voice of Dalit women, how they perceive Democratic Decentralization and how far it has helped them in constructing their identity. May I take this opportunity to congratulate the author for this excellent piece of work on issues related to Dalit women, his hard work, the intensive field work he has undertaken and brainstorming he has put in the analysis part to make this book a success.

Dr. Lekshmi V. Nair

Associate Professor, Department of Humanities
Indian Institute of Space Science and Technology (IIST)
Secretary Kerala Sociological Society (KSS)

Acknowledgements

There are many people who have contributed, in different ways, to the completion of this book. I am utmost grateful for the help and support I have received. I believe the following persons should enjoy recognition for offering their time and their assistance.

Special thanks to my mentor Dr. Jacob John Kattakayam, UGC Emeritus Professor, Dean Faculty of Social Sciences, Director cum Professor, Academic Staff College, University of Kerala. Member ICSSR, President Indian Sociological Society (Formerly) for your insightful ideas, comments and knowledge of development issues have been of great importance in producing this book.

My deepest regards to the interviewed women, who shared their experiences, their thoughts and who took time of their hands, in order to meet me. I hope this book can be as constructive for your individual situation, as your stories and experiences have been for my personal development.

I would be failing and become ungrateful if I do not place on records my sincere thanks to Dr. Lekshmi V. Nair Associate Professor, Department of Humanities, Indian Institute of Space Science and Technology (IIST) who took entire pains for going through the whole manuscript and writing a pertinent Foreword to this book.

Mr. John Christorpher (HSST Sociology) helped me to organize this book and I'm taking this opportunity to thank him for giving his valuable time for in-depth discussions in the midst of his busy schedules.

I deeply indebted to my better half Maniammal. K sons S. Karthik Ram and S. Koushik Lakshman for their perpetual support. Her encouraging companionship and creative suggestions, has made me more confident in pursuing my goal. I record my deep felt gratefulness to my beloved mother, sisters, and brothers who were always with me in all my visions.

–Author

Contents

Acronyms

BPL	–	Below Poverty Line
CDS	–	Community Development Society
DAC	–	District Advisory Committee
DPO	–	District Planning Officer
DRDA	–	Department of Rural Development Agency
GOI	–	Government Order of India
GP	–	Government Proceedings
HUDCO	–	Housing and Urban Development Corporation
HWD	–	Harijan Welfare Department
IAY	–	Indira Awas Yojana
ICDS	–	Integrated Child Development Services
IWEP	–	Integrated Women's Empowerment Programmes
JCP	–	Joint Parliamentary Committee of Parliament
JRY	–	Jawarhar Rozgar Yojana
JSS	–	Jan Sikshan Sansthan
KIRTADS	–	Kerala Institute for Research, Training and Development Studies of SCs and STs
KPRA	–	Kerala Panchayat Raj Act
LDF	–	Left Democratic Front
LPG	–	Liberalization Privatization and Globalization
LSG	–	Local Self Government
MLA	–	Member of Legislative Assembly
MWS	–	Million Wells Scheme
NABARD	–	National Agricultural Bank for Rural Development
NBCFDC	–	National Backward Classes Finance and Development Corporation
NBCFDC	–	National Backward Classes Finance and Development Corporation
NGOs	–	Non Governmental Organizations

NHGs – Neighbourhood Groups
NIPPCD – National Institute of Public Cooperation and Child Development
NMDFC – National Minorities Development and Finance Corporation
NSFDC – National Scheduled Caste Finance and Development Corporation
NSKFDC – National Safai Karamachars Finance Development Corporation
NSTFDC – National Scheduled Tribe Finance and Development Corporation
OBC Other Backward Community
PMGSY – Pradhan Mantri Gram Sadak Yojana
PPC – People's Plan Campaign
PRA – Participatory Rural Appraisal
PRIs – Panchayati Raj Institutions
RD – Rural Development
RLEGP – Rural Landless Employment Guarantee Programme
SCA – Special Central Assistance
SCDC – Scheduled Caste Development Officer
SCDD – Scheduled Caste Development Department
SCP – Special Component Plan
SCs – Scheduled Castes
SD – Standard Deviation
SGRY – Sampoorna Gramin Rozgar Yojana
SGSY – Swarnajayanti Gram Swarozgar Yojana
SHGs – Self Help Groups
SJPY – Sadhu Jena Paripalana Yogam
STED – Science and Technology Entrepreneurship Development
STEPW – Support Training and Employment Programme for Women
STs – Scheduled Tribes
WBM – Water Bound Macadam
WWS – Women's Welfare Services

1

Introduction

Gandhiji believed that India lives in villages and until and unless village life is revitalized it is hard for the nation to come alive. He advocated that the institutions of self-governmentfor the revitalization of the villages as it would strengthen the democratic freedoms in every village. He was of the opinion that the democracy in the post independent India should rely on the true participation of people in the planning and implementation processes of developmental and welfare activities through grass root level institutions. Gandhiji developed his idea of Panchayati Raj from the system of traditional Panchayats, the village republics. Due to the efforts of Dr. B.R. Ambedkar, the chief architect of our Constitutionthe village Panchayats was included in the State List of the Seventh Schedule. Article 234G of the Constitution, entrusts the panchayats with the responsibility of planning for social justice and economic development. Article 40 of the Constitution insists that 'The state shall take necessary actions to organize village Panchayats and to endow them with such powers and authority as may be necessary to enable them to function as units of self – government.' One of the major features of the powers and responsibilities of the Panchayats is DecentralisedPlanning. Decentralised planning fosters democratic participation of local people in the development of the community and to reduce the burden of top level administration. The democratic decentralisation process became widespread throughout the country following the 73rd amendment to the Constitution. However, one could see that the experience of the Panchayat Raj institutions is not uniform throughout the country. If some states have witnessed the empowerment of hitherto marginalized sections such as women, Scheduled Castes and Scheduled Tribes, in some other states the new system played a vital role in changing the traditional power structure dominated by local elites and bureaucratic networks (Bhandari, 2009).

The Decentralisation Process

Decentralisation is the process of diffusion of the decision making process close to the point of service or action. Manydisciplines such as engineering, management, science, political science, political economy, sociology and economics focus decentralisation as its main area of study. The concept has a Latin root that conveys the meaning 'away from the center" (Mac Mohan, 1961). It also implies the delegation of authority – legislative, judiciary or administrative from higher to lower levels of government (White, D-Leonord, 1959). It, therefore, invariably means the delegation of authority for planning, decision-making and administrative by the central government to the local bodies such as the field level organisations, local governments and non-government agencies. A democratic, deficient and viable decentralised administrative system with ever expanding functions of welfare and development is not only desirable but also necessary for the development of a country and is an essential dimension of modernization. To put it in another way, no meaningful development in the modern context is possible without decentralisation.

Development programmes are being implemented at different levels within the state. Organisations at an appropriate level are essential to coordinate, execute and supervise these programmes. The first level of decentralization trickles down from the state to districts. The Administration Reforms Commission recommended the districts to be the units of planning and hence, it should be the prime responsibility of the Zilla to formulate and implementthe central and state government schemes within the district.

Democratic Decentralisation: The Kerala Initiatives

Democratic decentralization is the establishment of local bodies, legally separated from the national center, with formal powers and responsibilities to decide upon a range of public matters to the people and their representatives. In democratic decentralization, peoples' representatives have local base and are given legislative mandate to take decisions that could be challenged or altered only through new legislations. It facilitates empowerment of the poor by ensuring their active participation in the local government institutions. Democratic decentralization has two merits in the present context – (i) consistent with the democratic trends; and (ii) the most efficient method of planning and implementing local development programmes. It provides opportunities for closer interaction between government officials and local people, the effective to way to ensures that local developmental problems are addressed properly. Efficient leadership is an essential condition for the effective functioning of the democratic decentralization system. Hence the fundamental aim in the Indian context should be to train local leadership to assume greater responsibilities so as to serve the people with efficiency and economy.

Empowerment of the poor is the broader objective of democratic decentralisation and decentralised planning. It has been recognized as the path through which critical needs of the people and unique circumstances that a central authority may fail to adhere to, could be effectively tackled.

For the poor, it opens the avenues to participate in politics and thus become participants in the decision making process that is expected to shape their future. Mobilisation of the poor which may lead the development process in such a way as to eradicate poverty, inequality and deprivations could be made possible (Rondinelli, 1983). Many developing countries have been successful in ensuring the participation of local people for improving the production and productive capacities. Participation in the decentralised democratic system is expected to bring about educative effects on people by enhancing civic consciousness and political maturity. Thus the process could be used as an effective mechanism to enhance people's participation in the development programmes that are directed to achieve sustainable livelihood security to people and an effective strategy to assert their political and economic power. It would also lead to the generation of well trained grassroots level political leaders.

The implementation of democratic decentralization was not an easy task in Kerala. It was in accordance with 73rd and 74th constitutional amendments and in conformity with the Acts of Kerala State and People's Plan Campaign for decentralization launched by the Left Democratic Front (LDF) Government that the process was initiated in 1996. However the efforts to implement democratic decentralisation in the state gave rise to a series of controversies, ideological debates and discussions. Controversies often crossed the limits and entered into personal attacks and mud-slinging. Ideological debates and discussions originated mainly from the leftists in Kerala who favoured a left-centre. However, whatsoever there was virtually little contribution from the leaders and supporters of the UDF and the congress (I) party in particular (Issac, T.M, 2000)

The effort towards democratic decentralisation in Kerala has a long history since the formation of the state. The Administrative Reforms Committee, appointed by the first democratically elected government headed by Sri. E.N Sankaran Namboodiripad, recommended a two-tier system of local government with Panchayat and Municipalities at the grass-root level and District government at the district level. With this aim The District Council Bill was introduced in the Kerala State Legislative Assembly in 1958. Unfortunately the bill did not come into limelight as the EMS government was dissolved in 1959 following its dismissal by the central government. However the second EMS government managed to get through the bill in 1969. Following this,the A.K Antony led Congress Ministry passed the Kerala District Administrative Bill in 1979 which was originally introduced in 1971 and re-introduced in 1978. Unfortunately the bill remained in the shelves until 1987 without any serious efforts to implement it. Finally, with the efforts of Sri E.K Nayanar, the LDF government (1987-91) took measures to implement the Act. Elections to the District Council were held in February 1990. The next UDF government headed by K. Karunakaran took back all the powers and responsibilities of District Councils in the very first meeting of the newly elected cabinet. Meanwhile, the central government came out with the 73rd and 74thamendments to the Constitution of India that provided constitutional status to the local bodies all over the country. Following this the Kerala Panchayat Raj act was enacted in 1994.

Though the act was progressive in nature, it required further strengthening to imbibe the spirit of democratic decentralization. With this aim the government of Kerala appointed a committed in July 1996 under the chairmanship of Dr. B.B. Sen from West Bengal to make recommendations on the decentralisation of powers. The committee submitted its interim report in 1996 and final report in 1997. The report contained recommendations for the amendment of the Kerala Panchayat Raj Act. Most of the recommendations were accepted and the amendment was effected in 1999. The duties and functions of the Local Self Government (LSG) were further broadened with these amendments.

The Kerala Panchayat Raj Act enlisted the duties and responsibilities of the village Panchayats. The act entrusted the responsibilities of collection of land revenue, maintenance of survey records, supervision and control of government primary schools, hospitals, public health, child welfare and maternity institutions and the implementation of community development programmes including improvement of agriculture, animal husbandry and village industries on the village Panchayat.

Even though the Kerala Panchayat Raj Act was concerned with village Panchayats ever since its enactment in 1960, several legislations were passed at the district level. The Kerala Panchayat Union Bill 1964, the Kerala Panchayat Raj Bill 1967 and the Kerala District Administration Bill 1979 were the major ones among them. But for several reasons the District Council as envisaged in the Act came into being only in 1991. But the Constitution Amendment of 1992 made its life short. Following the constitution amendment and the subsequent Kerala enactment the three tire system of Panchayats; village Panchayat at the village level, Block Panchayat at the intermediate level and District Panchayat at the district level, came into being with effect from 1st October 1995 with the due process of election to the three levels of panchayats.

Decentralisation: A means of Women Empowerment

The spirit of decentralization is the inclusion and involvement of all sections of peopleespecially the vulnerable sections of society like women and SC/STs in the various stages of development activities. Active participation in the decision making process in the socio-economic and political spheres would not only empower the vulnerable sections of society but also give women the desired self-respect and dignity which are the pre-requisites of empowerment.

The process of women empowerment would challenge the oppressive genderrelations existing within a patriarchal social system. This would change the traditional pattern of authority of men over women, especially over the household women. In communities where such changes have already occurred, women have already challenged the dominance of men over their bodies, sexuality and mobility. In such societies men cannot entrust the responsibilities of household work and child care solely on women. They cannot abuse women or treat them with impurity. They cannot abandon or divorce women without providing for maintenance or practice bigamy or polygamy or take unilateral decisions on behalf of the entire family.

Social status of women is a reliable index of social development. Unfortunately, women are treated as a neglected entity in almost all societies and throughout the ages. Women's unequal status and oppressive gender relations are embedded in the socio-cultural, political and economic history of every society. It is not because of their biological nature that women have to reconcile with their inferior status, rather they have been treated as subservient partners since generations and have always been deprived of participation in the political and decision-making processes (Archana, S and Shalu, N 2000). Various reasons may be attributed for the marginalization and oppression of women throughout the ages. Cultural practices and norms could be one among them. Strong cultural inhibitions along with the deeply embedded practice of patriarchy have made a devastating impact on the psyche of women. The situation has become so vulnerable that even the educated, employed and economically independent women alike the illiterate, uneducated rural poor women in the contemporary Indian society find it hard to liberate themselves from the clutches of male dominance and have to remain psychologically and socially dependent on their male counter parts, be it father, husband or son.

Family being the primary cell of social organisation, the role women perform with its context is of great significance in nation building. Future of any nation depends upon the quality of children who are born and brought up within the family especially by women. One cannot neglect the fact that children hailing from broken families more often become a menace to the society and hinter the nation building process. Therefore, we could say that, women's most enduring contribution towards nation building begins at home, though it does not end there (Anuradha, Sharma, 1998). It is, therefore, imperative that customs, traditions, rituals, values and attitudes that consider women as oppressed be discarded or changed and necessary steps be taken to provide the much needed encouragement, support, opportunities and facilities both within and outside home so as to enable them to combine efficiently and successfully their different roles as home-makers, mothers and as socially productive individuals. This necessitates the urgency to carry out more researches works to bring into limelight the socio-economic conditions and problems faced by women of various categories.

In most traditional societies women are treated as second grade citizens, whose every aspect of life is confined to the rigid restrictions imposed by caste, customs and traditions as envisaged in religious texts and social customs. Our religions and social customs insist that women have to be confined within the home and be prohibited from receiving education or pursuing any profession, trade or occupation of their choice and social participation. To say it differently, there is social injection, implicit in our social and religious customs that strictly prohibits Indian women from participating in any activities outside home, be it social, literary or professional (Chitkara, M. G, 2001). Though efforts have been made in our constitution and through other legislation to promote gender equality, status of women continues to be low. Empowerment of women is the solution to this problem. This implies women gain control and power over their own lives. It can be achieved through awareness building, promoting self-confidence, expansion of choices, increased access to and control over resources. The impetus to promote women empowerment should come from within the women folk and it should facilitate the articulation of their needs and priorities and taking more active role in promoting these needs and interests. The gender mainstreaming strategy, evolved in the 1980s and adopted by most of the countries across the world, is aimed at making the goal of gender equality central to all development activities. In our country too there is a great upsurge in the awareness about women's rights among all sections of society. Our development programmes and policies give special emphasis for improving the status of women. Our development efforts enabled women to double their life expectancy over the last fifty years or so along with a considerable reduction in infant and child mortality rates (Remesh, 2003). Indian economy and culture being predominantly agrarian and rural, empowering women who are the backbone of our agrarian economy is a sure path to achieve major economic gains.

Empowerment: A Rereading of the Concept

The concept 'empowerment' originated from the theoretical and practical debates as well as from the experiences of women working at the grass-root levels in many parts of the world. Enabling approach, i.e., enabling people to identify and express their needs and priorities, captured the attention of development agencies in 1990's when the terms like participation, consultation and partnership entered the development thinking. The notion 'empowerment' arose in this context.

The dictionary meaning of the term empowerment is to give power to, to give capacity to perform some physical or mental activity, to delegate authority, to give legal rights, to enable or to entitle to endow (invest) with powers.

In literature different terminologies with divergent emphasis and agendas are used in discussions on women empowerment. Though the concepts such as 'women's empowerment', 'gender equality', 'female autonomy', and 'women's quality' are used synonymously, they actually differ considerably. The concept 'women empowerment' can be distinguished from the above terms by two essential elements. The first is the process; none of the other terms explicitly emphasis a progression from one state (gender inequality) to another (gender equality). The second element is agency; the situation in which women themselves are significant actors in the process of change that is being described or measured. Thus, hypothetically there could be improvement in the status of women by ensuring gender equality, but unless the intervening process involved women as agents of such change rather than mere recipients, it cannot be considered as empowerment. However desirable, it could only mean an improvement in outcomes from one stage to another.

Empowerment is either referred to as a goal, as is the case with many development projects or as a process that people undergo, that eventually leads to change. For Nelly Stromquist empowerment is "a process to change the distribution of power both in interpersonal relations and in institutions throughout society", whereas Lucy Lazo defines it as "a process of acquiring, providing, bestowing the resources and the means for enabling the access to control over such means and resources" (Rao and Latha, 1998). The second definition implies that either the individual acquires power through self-initiatives orthe power is imparted by another individual. This indicates that the potential agent of empowerment could be either the individual herself or another person or agent. In this sense empowerment could be a self-propelled or a propelling process.

An empowered individual will be able to judge the desirability of the current situation, perceive a better situation and visualize the possibilities of realizing it. This implies that that the empowerment is a process that involves a change of perception about the self, the environment and the relationship of the self with the environment. It is the process that involves the creating of images and the generation of a push to act or 'motivation' as referred by the psychologists. Change of perception involves a change of one's attitude and outlook towards oneself and the social situation. In the case of women, empowerment enables them to generate choices and as an outcome of such choices, gainleverage and bargaining power. Empowered women would take initiatives to find or generate options or means to find the options. When one is handy with options, one may (a) choose not to follow the pressure and demands of the more powerful party and; (b) ask and negotiate with the other party to change the situation and make it more amicable. Thus empowerment enables a person to demand and exercise choice. It endows the individual with the capability to fix her goals, generate opportunities to pursue it and determine the overall direction of one's life thus making the notion of empowerment a fascinating and powerful one (Venkatakrishnan, J, 2001).

The term empowerment is more significant in the case of the marginalized, the poor, the illiterate, the indigenous communities, and of course, women in general. Very often the term is used as a substitute for the development, uplift, participation and conscientisation of women. But in fact, empowerment is not synonymous to these terms; rather it is broader a concept.

Power: A Key Element of Empowerment

The literal meaning of empowerment is centered on the concept of power. 'Power is the ability of one person or group to get another person or group to do something against their will'. Parsons is of the opinion that as power becomes legitimate, there is no end to its development and therefore power need not be a zero sum game in which there is winners and losers (Parsons, Tn1963). Power has the following four dimensions.

Power Over

Power in the social, economic and political realms provides control over resources and decision making. The perception, preferences and choices of a group are determined by the ability to exercise power by one over another (Rowlands, 1997). Srilatha Batliwala defines power as 'control over resources, ideology and self, exercised in the social, economic and political contexts'. Resources comprise of physical, human and financial. Control over ideology indicates the ability to determine beliefs, values and attitudes. Exercising thinking power, self-image, self-confidence and articulation are the signs of control over self. The extent of power an individual holds would depend on the longitude and latitude of resources they have access to and control over which in turn endows with the power to decision making (Batliwala, S 1995).

Power within

Power within represents the power that is present within the individual in different degrees which include spiritual strength, self-esteem and assertiveness (Rowlands, 1997). It is important to nurture power within in order to overcome the internalized feelings of subordination. This power enables each individual to take necessary steps to analyse one's situation, make decisions and foster change.

Power with

Power with is all about support, solidarity and collaboration. It strengthens those who are disempowered as well as those who already hold power such as the elite groups like lobbies that support each other.

Power to

Through the 'power to' one acquires the ability to negotiate and make decisions that will generate new possibilities for one. This is acquired by becoming aware of our interests through the power within/with (Eyben, R 2004). This power will guard us against the acquisition of false consciousness. 'Power to' is also about the ability to generate power in others. 'Power within' and 'power to' combined together perform the role of agency. In short the 'power to' enables us either as individuals or members of a group, to be significant actors in shaping and changing the world in a way better suited to satisfy our own interests.

For NailaKabeer, the core of empowerment is the idea of gaining power and this idea is central to many theories. As she clearly indicates, the concept of empowerment is clearly rooted in the notion of power and in its reverse powerlessness or the absence of power (Kabeer, N 1994). Power can emerge from many sources such as what one knows and how one applies what she knows. It can also come from one's status, background, strength or intelligence. Power may also be bestowed on one by an external source or it may be self-acquired.

Measuring Empowerment

Empowerment is a term generally used to describe a process by which people without power become conscious of their own situation and organises collectively to gain greater access to public services and benefits of economic growth. There is no single criterion to measure it. However, it could be understood and defined in terms of certain indicators such as personal, social, economic and political changes.

Empowerment implies the ability to influence the direction of social change towards a more egalitarian social and economic order (Batliwala, 1995). Empowerment can be understood (i) in relation to the poor or the powerless; and (ii) empowerment of women. Paulo Frier for the first time mentioned the term in his theories by using the concept 'conscientisation', as a process by which the poor could challenge the structure of power and take control of their lives. However he ignored gender while talking about power. Feminists expanded Frierian empowerment analysis by incorporating gender dimension to it (Batliwala, S 1995).

Components and Dimensions of Empowerment

Most of the literature on empowerment emphasizes resources and agency (in various forms and by various means like control, awareness, voice and power) as its most common components. Some cases consider resources as catalysts for empowerment, as enabling factors of empowerment process rather than empowerment itself. Many of the variables that have traditionally been used as 'proxies' for empowerment, such as education and empowerment, might be better described as 'enabling factors', 'resources' or 'sources' of empowerment. Another component, agency, is the heart of many conceptualizations of empowerment. It encompasses the ability to formulate strategic choices and to control resources and decisions that affect important life outcomes.

The flow chart represents the major dimensions of empowerment.

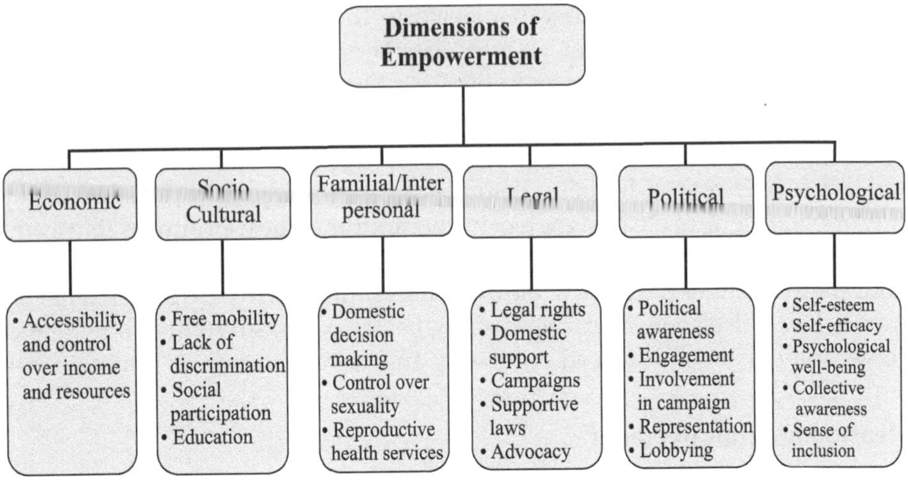

Some propositions for Women Empowerment

Some propositions that will enable women to achieve individual and collective empowerment are cited below.

- The extent to which women are independent in their families where the seeds of empowerment are sown.
- The extent to which women can develop their own beliefs and practices. Belief in a supreme being can empower women in the search for survival and fulfillment.
- Mutual support in work settings in and outside home is vital to women's empowerment, in that they see their own historical and cultural circumstances.
- Having aware of the broader world context to their lives empowers women in their own historical and cultural circumstances.
- To the extent that individual women connect their biographies with history, seeing the influence of broad social structures on their lives.

Women's mutual support though necessary is not a sufficient condition for their empowerment. A woman alone cannot fully develop her potential or make her contributions to society in the fullest sense (Suguna, B 2001).

Towards Women Empowerment

A prerequisite of women empowerment is stepping outside home and participation in some form of collective undertakings. This would facilitate the development of independence, competency, self-esteem and autonomy of women and boost the process of their goal attainment. Whatever be the objective; creation of small, cohesive groups is paramount as the small scale and voluntary nature of these associations will enable its members to gain valuable experience and confidence in both leadership and membership tasks. The groups may undertake any of the diverse forms of action such as; literacy, income generation, satisfaction of basic needs or support.

Empowerment will necessarily take a series of phases. Awareness building at personal and collective levels is the beginning which will automatically lead to some form of public action which will in turn reflect in the role assertion of women within the family and eventually place more demands upon the state.

Departure, knowledge attainment, economic leverage and political mobilization are the different ways for attaining women empowerment. Even though, very often, the work women perform outside their home to support their family are exhausting and meagerly rewarded, access to income gives them a better say at home. Working women, regardless of the position in their work place or size of the income they earn, are more powerful, exercise greater sense of control over their own lives and resources within the family than non-working women.

In order to be empowered women must:

- develop a sense of independence. Although many women would like to be protected, sooner or later women must address the issue of becoming independent and make choices in one direction oranother.
- choose to develop ones potential as it is synonymous to the choices to be empowered.
- overcome problems in all stages of life cycle.
- choose to lead a meaningful life. Women must be courageous to ask basic questions about the quality of their lives in order to live fully and productive.
- face the facts of their lives at all levels of social organization (Narasimhan, S 2000).

The accomplishment of women's empowerment does not mean that others will necessarily live oppressed.Whenwomen choose to be empowered; they are in a stronger position to support others and make substantial contributions to society.

The Empowerment Framework

The core of women empowerment rests on the vitality of its elements. The levels of women empowerment according to Tongue (Year???) are welfare, access, conscientisation, participation and control. This framework provides an overall view progress in women empowerment.

Welfare

Provision of welfare services would enable women to address the basic need of solving the structural problems. At this point, women act the role of passive beneficiaries.

Access

This level involves ensuring equality of access to resources such as education, land and credit. The path of empowerment is cleared when women realize the lack of access to resources as a barrier to their growth and development and initiate necessary action to address it (Suguna, B 2001). In short, access to resources is an essential condition to make meaningful progression in the process of women empowerment.

Conscientisation

Conscientisation is a critical step in the empowerment framework. Empowerment of women depends on the awareness that gender discrimination is not accidental; but systematic and structural. Women must also become aware of the role they can play in breaking this structured inequality.

Participation

This is the point where women become co-participants in the decision making process with men. Mobilization, organization and collective effort will enable them to gain better representation in the decision making process.

Control

Control is the ultimate level of equality achieved through empowerment. In this stage women achieve a status that is equal to men and neither party dominates over the other. At this level womenareempowered in such a way as to take decisions over their lives and lives of their children and play an active role in the process of development.

Empowerment frame work enables development planners to determine the level to be focused by the project or programme; welfare, access, conscientisation, participation or control and fix points of intervention so that women can move further towards equality and empowerment. An empowerment approach to development can also mean peoples' participation in the policy making and implementation processes. Empowerment follows a spiral process that helps to chart a broader activity schedule for the national, regional and global level agencies with women participation in focus.

Empowerment through Women Collectives

Women organizations and their community participation are the effective ways of women empowerment, poverty eradication and assertion of their entitlement to various services related to their socio-economic wellbeing.

Women require training in establishing organizations, undertaking essential social services and promotional programmes, availing credit and loan facilities, family and primary health care and leadership skills. A participatory approach in these areas would enable them to articulate their hopes and aspirations by becoming participants in various programmes as effective partners. In India different voluntary organizations have successfully implemented this strategy. Several women acquired a sense of dignity and confidence to tackle their problems along with economic independence through this participatory group process. This enabled women to improve their standard of living and secure small capital assets (Agarwal, D 2001).

Significance of Women Empowerment

Women empowerment ultimately aims at a new world devoid of subordination based on sex. Empowered women will have control over their labour, income, sexuality, reproduction and mobility as well as challenge the prevailing stereotyped gender roles, division of labour and related oppressive systems. They would transform themselvesfrom being submissive to be articulate and questioning, educated, challenging the gendered division of labour and ensure their free mobility. Their earnings and control over their income ensure economic independence for women and gain confidence in facing problems individually or in collectivities. Empowered women will acquire a global vision and will be able to see issues from a wider perspective, allowing them to analyse the personal problems from a political angle. Collective empowerment would enable them to socialize their children in a gender sensitive manner and make them powerful enough to shift the direction of development towards women oriented one; thus ensure the advancement of the society at large.

The Plight of Indian Women and measures taken for their Empowerment

Development of any country depends on the socio-economic and political empowerment of its citizens especially the women folk. Gender equality is the key to empowerment. Most of the developing countries have made their progress through the empowerment of women which generally reflects in the literacy, health and economic wellbeing of families (Gupta, K.N 2001).

The Government of India declared 2001 as the 'Year of Women Empowerment'. Through empowerment, women will be able to develop self-esteem, confidence, recognize their potential and enhance their collective bargaining power. This is achieved through the interplay of several interrelated and mutually reinforcing components. Undoubtedly, we have a long way to go to achieve this end.

Women in our country continue to be in the lower social strata due to the lack of awareness about their rights, illiteracy and oppressive practices and customs. This is manifested in the areas such as constant fall in sex ratio, low literacy, high drop-out and low wage rates of women. Acknowledging this the Seventh Five year Plan emphasized 'women empowermentthrough awareness building and instilling confidence in them about their rights and privileges so as to integrate them in the nation-building process as equal partners' (Gupta, K.N 2001).

In par with the constitution, the State has undertaken legal measures for women empowerment by ensuring equal rights and protection from discrimination, atrocities and human right violations and to ensure support services especially to working women. Section 2 of the Protection of Human Rights Act, 1993 defines 'human rights' as the rights relating to life, liberty, equality and dignity of the individual guaranteed by the Constitution or embodied in the International Covenants enforced by the courts in India. 'International Covenants' include the International Covenant on civil and political rights and International Covenants on economic, social and cultural rights adopted by the General Assembly of the UN on the 16th of December 1966. Let us have a look at some of the measures adopted by India for women empowerment.

Parliamentary Committee on the Empowerment of Women: A Joint Parliamentary Committee (JPC) was constituted on 09/04/1997 with the objective of securing dignity and equality for women in all fields.

National Commission for Women: It is a statutory body set up on 31/10/1992 in accordance with the National Commission for Women Act, 1990. The commission strives to achieve equity, equality and justice for women in India. It tries to ensure gender justice by intervening in cases where women suffer from discrimination, deprivation and denial of opportunities. It provides counselling services to women victims and to women who are in distress.

Protection of Human Rights Act, 1993 and the National Human Rights Commission: Protection and promotion of human life with dignity is the heart and soul of this act and commission. The act and the commission envisage ensuring freedom from hunger and illiteracy that are essential to the right to live with dignity. The commission emphasized that promotion of human rights and expansion of essential freedoms must be the central purpose of governance.

The Convention on the Elimination of all forms of Discrimination against Women: It is one of the United Nation's women's rights instruments. The Convention invoked the State Parties to take appropriate measures including legislations to ensure the full development and advancement of women, enable them to enjoy their rights and fundamental protection from gender discrimination in all areas, particularly, political, social, economic and cultural fields. State Parties may take measures to ensure equal rights to women in the fields of education, employment, access to health care including family planning measures and in other areas of economic and social life (Narayanan, K.S 1998).

The Convention of Political Rights of Women: This is one of the important international instruments that ensure political rights to women. The articles of the convention entitle women with; the rights to vote in all elections, eligibility to get elected to all public elected bodies established by National Law, entitlement to hold public office and access to all public functions on equal terms with men without any discrimination.

The Convention for the suppression of the Traffic in persons and of the Exploitation of the Prostitution of others: As per the agreement in the convention, any act to gratify the passion of another person; procuring, enticing or leading for prostitution and exploiting another person's sexuality even with the person's consent is punishable. The parties agree, through their educational, health, socio-economic and other related services, to encourage measures for the prevention of prostitution and rehabilitation of the victims.

The Convention on the Nationality of Married Women: As per this Convention, neither the celebration nor the dissolution of a marriage between individuals from two nationalities or the change of nationality by the bridegroom during the marriage shall have an automatic impact on the nationality of the bride. The acquisition or renouncement of a particular nationality by the husband is not supposed to impose restriction on the change of nationality of the wife.

Department for Women and Child Development: It is a nodal department that strives to secure gender equality through a wide coverage of programmes. The department aims at adopting measures to ensure women equal property rights, credit and income generating opportunities and other support services. Day care services, crèches and working women's hostels are being run by the Department. It also organizes women self-help groups and cooperative societies and runs programmes for awareness generation and gender sensitization. Some other initiatives of the Government under the influence of the Department include; observation of 'Women's empowerment Year' in 2001, Integrated Child Development Services (ICDS), Reproductive Child and Health Programme, Balika Samridhi Yojana scheme, Component Plan for Women, Swashakli project, Plan of Action to Combat Trafficking and Commercial Sexual Exploitation of Women and Children, National Policy for Empowerment of Women, Parliamentary Committee for empowerment of Women, Rashtriya Mahila Kosh and the National Institute of Public Cooperation and Child Development (NIPPCED).

Central Social Welfare Board: The activities of the Central Social Welfare Board include promoting social welfare activities for the general public such as; welfare of family, women, children and the differently abled; rendering technical and financial aid to deserving institutions; setting up and promoting voluntary organizations in places where they do not exist and organizing emergency relief measures at times of calamity.

The major thrust all these programmes has been women empowerment through capacity building, providing condensed courses of education and vocational training; economic empowerment through assistance to agrobased production units, support services like working women's hostels, counselling centers and awareness generation programmes.

Ever since the UN Declaration of the 'Decade of Women' in 1975, actions and programmes on women related issues are steadily on the increase. Women's organizations, government agencies and international donor agencies are giving special emphasis to education, consciousness building and skills acquisition of women. The underlying assumption was that if women are aware of their conditions, knew their rights and learned skills traditionally denied to them, their empowerment would follow.

Dalit: Assertion of an Identity

The term 'Dalit' meaning 'the deprived' has its origin in Pali language. Dalit Panthers, a radical movement of Scheduled Caste youth used this term for the first time as a symbol of their confident assertion by rejecting the nomenclature of Harijan, the name given by Mahatma Gandhi. Initially the word comprised of the Scheduled Castes and Scheduled Tribes, neo-Budhists, the working people, the landless and the poor peasants, women and all those who were exploited socially, politically and economically and in the name of religion. The term does not represent any particular cast; it symbolizes unity of all those who suffered at the hands of the Brahminical supremacy, the basis of Hindutva. The term is often used as symbol of change and revolution. Believing in humanism, Dalits reject the existence of god, rebirth and soul, denounce the sacred books that teach discrimination, fate and the concepts of hell and heaven, as all these beliefs were unfavoruable to them. At present the word is used in a narrower sense referring only to the untouchable (socially excluded) and Adivasi (geographically excluded) communities.

The Demographic Profile of Dalits in India

As per the census of 2001 the Scheduled Caste and Scheduled Tribes together constituted 24.4 per cent of India's population (16.2% SC and 8.2% ST). Numerically it was 166.67 million and 84.32 million for SCs and STs respectively (the figures exclude the SC/STs in the state of Jammu and Kashmir). Dalits, though numerically powerful, remain an oppressed community even today.

The census data further reveals that the sex ratio among the SCs is 936,which is slightly higher than the national average of 933. The largest proportion of the Scheduled Castes to total population of the State is found in Punjab (28.9 per cent) followed by Himachal Pradesh (24.7 percent) and West Bengal (23 percent). In Andhra Pradesh, Karnataka and Pondicherry proportion of SCs' population is exactly the same as the National average of

16.2 per cent. The smallest concentration of the Scheduled Castes population is found in the north-eastern states of Mizoram (as negligible as 272 persons) followed by Meghalaya (0.5 per cent) and Arunachal Pradesh (0.6 per cent). The highest percentage of Scheduled Castes population to the total SCs population of the country is reported in Uttar Pradesh (21.1 per cent) followed by West Bengal (11.1 per cent), Bihar (7.8 per cent), Andhra Pradesh (7.4 percent) and Tamil Nadu (7.1.percent). In fact, more than 57 per cent of the total SC population inhabit in these five States. There are only 22 districts where the SC population is 30 per cent or more.

The Socio-economic Situation of Dalits

The social injustice, cultural and economic deprivation and exclusion faced by these sections have a historical legacy. Caste system within the Hindu society gave special privileges and powers to the upper castes in the cultural, social, economic, political, legal and administrative fields including the right for upananya, the initiation ceremony for education and acquisition of knowledge. Whereas the rights for; education and gaining knowledge, vocation of choice of occupation and good habitation, the three principal needs for human development were legally denied to the Dalits and Adivasis. Until the advent of the British period there was hardly any social and occupational mobility amongst the Shudras. Capitalism brought about by colonialism brought certain fundamental changes in the economic structure of Indian society. For the first time crime and punishment were delinked from caste and social status. Private property established through the legal ownership and tenancy resulted in the emergence of individuals in every caste who could gain education, land ownership and access to new opportunities. Even though some individuals from the lower castes benefitted from the new opportunities, it did not give much leverage for lower castes in general. The new elite and middle class created by the colonial rule was primarily drawn from the upper castes. Hence one can rightly say that the colonial rule actually tended to strengthen the then existed unequal distribution of resources. Independent India inherited the same social, legal and administrative structure of the colonial pastwith upper cast domination in all spheres. The new economic and social order in post-independent India paved the way for further consolidation and strengthening of the hold of the upper castes.

Despite the fact that 'Untouchability' has been legally abolished right from the adoption of Indian constitution in 1956, the practice of imposing social disabilities on persons by reasons of birth continues very much a part of rural India. In some parts of the country the 'Untouchables' are prohibited from entering the geographical area inhabited by the higher castes. In many villages they may not use the same wells used by the upper castes, visit the same temples, drink from the same cups in the tea stalls or establish claim on their legitimate property. Dalit children are often made to sit at the back in class rooms. Most Dalits continue to live in absolute poverty without land or opportunities for better occupation or education and are often forced to perform degrading rituals in the name of caste. With an exception of a minority who have benefitted from the policy of reservation in government jobs and education, most of them are engaged in menial jobs such as scavengers, removers of human waste and dead animals, leather workers, street sweepers and cobblers. Dalit children make up the majority of those who are being sold into bondage to pay off debts to up upper caste creditors. Tens of millions of Dalit men, women and children work as agricultural labourers for meager rewards like few kilograms of rice or rupees 15 to 35 a day. Caste is often used as a cover to safeguard the exploitative economic arrangements and to provide social sanction for the lower status of the Dalits allowing their impoverishment to persist.

Dalits: The Scheduled Castes

Scheduled Casts are the ex-untouchables, who continue to follow the Hindu faith (D'Souza, 1983). The word 'Caste' is derived from the Portuguese word 'casta' meaning 'breed, race or kind'. The Portuguese during the eleventh century used the term indiscriminately to denote the different social and occupational groups found in the subcontinent. The term is now used in two different contexts: to describe the entire system of stratification found in Indian society; or to denote some distinct aspects of this system of stratification such as varna, jati and gotra (Chatterjee, 1996). SCs are those castes that are included in the Government of India SCs order promulgated in August 1950 (Santhakumari, 1982). In this context an individual is considered a member of SC if he/she belongs to a caste which, under the constitution, has been declared to be SC for that area in which he/she resides (Brochure, 1988). Only the President of India is authorized to declare a caste to be SC and the list can only be amended through an act in the Parliament (Chandra, 1981). The term 'Scheduled Caste' was first used in the Government of India Act 1935. The purpose of the classification was to safeguard the interests of such castes and provide them special concessions to enable them to catch up with the rest of the society in the process of development. The criteria used to consider a cast as SC are: (i) low position in Hindu social structure, (ii) educational backwardness, (iii) inadequate representation in government services, (iv) inadequate representation in trade, commerce and industry and (v) social and physical isolation from the rest of the society (Parvathamma, 1984).

Dalit Women in India's Caste Based Social System

The Dalit women are laden with a triple levels of burden imposed by caste, class and gender which highlights the fact that Dalit women are a distinct social group who cannot be masked under the general categories of 'women' or 'Dalits'.The hardships, the Dalit women are doomed to face,are not simply the product of their economic status, poverty or lack of education alone;but are the direct outcomes of the severe exploitation and suppression imposed by the upper classes, legitimized by the Hindu sacred texts (Agarwal, S 1992). Women identity itself imposes a lot of restrictions in terms of access, ownership, control and use of community resources. The situation is further aggravated when the social stigma of Dalit identity is added to it. In a matriarchal society Dalit women are exposed to unimaginable and inescapable oppression in the label of caste and gender. These forms of oppression and suppression of Dalit women continue to survive in the contemporary society.

As per the records of the National Commission on SC and ST, approximately 75% of Dalit girls drop out from primary school despite the fact that reservations for Dalit children is strictly imposed by the Government of India (National Commission for Scheduled Caste and Scheduled Tribe, Government of India, 2000). Poverty, humiliation, bullying and isolation by the classmates, society and even by the teachers are the major reasons for this gigantic rate of drop outs among the Dalit girls. The print and visual media along with the government reports bring out a number of atrocities on Dalit women on a daily basis (Thind, G 1999). It is also to be born in mind that thousands of such cases are left unreported as the poor Dalit victims in rural areas have no control over power, wealth, justice, police and the media.

Even after seventy years of India's independence and strong laws in place to protect Dalit women, they are still being victimized to unimaginable atrocities. Education is the only way out for this folk to come out of this vicious circle of poverty, abuse and oppression. Education would make them aware of their basic human rights and would empower them to raise their voice against abuse and exploitation from others (Agarwal, S 1992).

Women in general are a depressed class in India. Scheduled caste women are the most neglected sections among them as they traditionally possess inferior status compared to their counter parts in other communities. However, the recent socio-political changes and government efforts have opened up new avenues of opportunities for education and employment for these women. As traditional barriers to social mobility have been eliminated, they are now more exposed to occupational choices that are expected to open up entry in all walks of life. Modernization along with the opportunities for education and occupation gave impetus for the social mobility of scheduled caste women in India (Viswanath, V 1993).

The Situation of Scheduled Caste Women in Kerala

In Kerala, the scheduled caste women are a stigmatized category and they suffer from a number of disabilities that are strengthened by religion. They suffer from untouchability, segregation, low economic status, politically powerlessness, low level of educational attainment, little chance of mobilization and so on. All these factors are mutually reinforcing and worsen the situation of scheduled caste women. Though legally and constitutionally they are no more 'untouchables', in practice many of them still bear this stigma.

The scheduled castes in Kerala bear the anguish and burden of a long and unbroken legacy of the deepest social degradation. In general, they fall at the bottom in terms of any parameters of economic wellbeing and quality of life. The distinct burden only they bear, among all under privileged groups in Kerala, is the degradation caused by the centuries old tradition of untouchability. Even the tribals, who have lived in almost complete isolation from the mainstream civilization, society and economyuntil recently, are not exposed to this tragic situation.

Apart from the common disabilities imposed by the religious institutions, the SC women in Kerala were exposed to the vulnerabilities of restricted social mobility, forced labour and restrictions on normal social privileges. Their status remains low irrespective of the area they live – rural or urban. Traditionally they experienced bitter treatment from the hands of the upper castes, denied education and were forced to follow specific habits, customs and ways of life that were entirely different from those followed by the higher caste women. Literacy rate among the scheduled castes in general and scheduled caste women in particular had been the lowest in Kerala. They were doomed to serve as agricultural labourers and forced to perform other manual jobs such as scavenging that do not require any formal education.

Continuous efforts from the part of the government through welfare measures, provision of education and job opportunities along with the efforts of social leaders and reformers have helped them to improve their image and status in the contemporary society. Efforts from the part of the government along with the emergent socio-economic developments created new attitudes and aspirations among SC women. Education is given due emphasis as a powerful tool for improving the subordinate position of SC women. All these enabled to take a long leap in the status and style of life of SC women compared to the earlier period.

Problems faced by SC Women

The SCs occupy the lowest position in the traditional caste hierarchy which exposes them to a number of disabilities and disadvantages. They were denied education and forced to engage in manual occupations such as agricultural labour, tattooing and collecting firewood from the forest. SC women all over India have several handicaps for leading a normal social life.

The central and state governments have adopted various measures for the uplift of SCs. Accordingly several Acts and policies have been passed, deliberate attempts through welfare programmes have been made, numerous facilities have been provided; all with a view to enable them to take their rightful place in society. Through five year plans, targets have been laid down for the improvement of the social conditions of SCs in general and SC women in particular. The living conditions of these sectionshave, to some extent, improvedthrough the state interventions over the years since independence. Prohibition of untouchability, ensuring temple entry, access to public places and other legal measure are important steps in this direction. Undoubtedly some degree of social and economic mobility has been achieved through these measures. There is noticeable improvement in many areas such as education, occupation and other socio-cultural fields. In spite of these concerted efforts and achievements the conditions of the scheduled castes especially the women folk continue to be worse. There are various reasons for this backwardness.

Table 1.1: District wise distribution of scheduled caste population in Kerala in 2001

District	Total Population	Male	Female	% of Female Total Population
Kasargod	90218	44904	45314	50.23
Kannur	98991	48275	50716	51.23
Wayanad	33364	16738	16626	49.83
Kozhikode	200983	98386	102597	51.05
Malappuram	285442	140535	114907	50.76
Palakkad	432578	210624	221954	51.31
Thrissur	354226	171443	182783	51.60
Ernakulam	263518	129706	133812	50.78
Iddukki	159362	79389	79973	50.18
Kottayam	150282	73885	76397	50.83
Alappuzha	199231	96900	102331	51.36
Pathanamthitta	162002	78731	83271	51.40
Kollam	322887	156880	166007	51.41
Thiruvananthapuram	370857	178718	192139	51.81
Kerala	3123941	1525114	1598827	51.18

Source: www.censuskerala.org

The scheduled castes never appeared to have been the owners of means of production; even if they happened to be, the extent of their acquisition was only meager. The vast majority of them probably suffers from the disabilities and fall prey to atrocities in the hands of the owner classes in many parts of the country. They still experience the lack of skill in occupational mobility, ownership of land, housing, etc. Most of them are employed in agriculture and similar unorganized sectors. The development strategy of the post Independent India has its base on capital intensive industrialization. The unskilled SC population especially their women folk are unable to catch up with this kind of capital intensive development. Government policies over the years focused on extending welfare measures to them. Unfortunately, the policy makers did not pay much attention on the skill development of these sections, resulting in little or few programmes being implemented with this orientation. Thus one can rightly say that the policies followed by the governments in the post independent period contributed its due share in aggravating the situation of the SC women and alienating them from the mainstream.

Caste system is presumably the major factor that influences all aspects of Indian society, viz., social and economic interactions, distribution of opportunities for education, ownership of land, employment and administrative positions leading to the backwardness of the SCs. Both colonial administration as well as democratic government in independent India equally failed to make much advancement in the direction of changing the social stigma attached to the depressed sections. Drive for the political empowerment of Dalits is in its initial stages as it remains largely at the mercy of the mainstream national or regional political parties. A Dalit or subaltern perspective is slow to develop in India for many reasons. Part of the problem has been the slow development of mass education and continued upper caste monopoly over communication and culture. Failures to effectively implement land reforms and to ensure a decentralised political system are the other major reasons. Due to all these reasons a major chunk of the SC population particularlySC women, mostly living in rural India, are doomed to continue at the bottom of the socio-economic ladder.

In Keralaalso the scenario is not quite different. However the factors such as improvement in the level of education, opportunities for modern occupation, wider inter caste contacts and development of modern attitude towards social issues have opened up ways for the social mobility of SCs in general and women in particular. The census reports and the reports of the Commissioner of SC and ST provide some yardsticks to measure the changes in the demographic and educational fields. But no systematic and scientific efforts have been made so far to identify the factors responsible for and the rate of social mobility among the SC women in Kerala. Hence the present study is intended to assess the social mobility of SC women by comparing their occupational, economic and educational backgrounds along with their levels of aspiration and attitudes with the prevalence of different social issues faced by two generations of SC women. The findings of this study are expected to strengthen our current knowledge about this community and in giving useful information to the planners and policy makers engaged in the uplift of SC women.

2

Methodology

Statement of the Problem

The development discourse in the contemporary period has taken a shifted from the traditional trickle down approach to the modern bottom-up approach with special focus on people's participation. The democratic decentralisation through Panchayat Raj Institutions India is one such approach that ensures people's participation in planning and execution of development at local levels. In Kerala, the process takes an inclusive phase by involving cross-sections of the people including women and backward sections in the decision making and development processes. But, in spite of this formal constitutional mechanism, women's participation and empowerment are said to be unsatisfactory all over the country. Among the SC women, the condition is more deplorable owing to their lower placement in the socio-economic hierarchy.

Socio-politically women became visible in large numbers at the local levels only with the enactments of the 73rd and 74th Constitutional Amendments, which mandated 33 percent representation of women at all the three levels of the PRIs. With the amendments, a conscious attempt is made to incorporate gender issues into this process of decentralised planning. The PRIs were advised to set apart 10 percent of the plan grant from the state for preparing projects that directly benefit women. 73rd and 74th amendments, thus, are certainly a revolutionary step in the direction of socio-political emancipation of women. In the predominantly patriarchal social set up women rarely had any say in the decision-making process within and outside the families in any field, be it social, cultural, economic, or political. However, the conditions of women belonging to different socio-economic and cultural strata were not necessarily of uniform in nature.

A prerequisite to women empowerment necessitates stepping out of home and participate in some form of collective undertakings which would enable to develop a sense of self dependence and competence among the women folk. Thus, creation of small, cohesive groups with which its members may identify closely, is important. Because of face-to-face and voluntary nature of the association, members gain valuable experience and confidence in both leadership and their tasks in the group. The activities in the groups are designed in such a way as its process and goal attainment foster the development of a sense of self-esteem, competence and autonomy. While, many work outside homes to support their families, access to income improves their authority within the home. Working women, regardless of their inferior position and little income, enjoy; more freedom, greater sense of control over their lives, more power as well as control over resources within the family than nonworking women.

But the conditions of women living in the rural areas are worse when compared to those in the urban areas. In India, 70 percent of the rural women, especially from the SC categories who constitute the most depressed sections in the Indian social structure, are leading a deplorable life. Within the SC community itself, women have been placed in the lowest row of its hierarchal ladder.

Kerala stands unique in most of the socio-demographic indicators like; the female literacy, life-expectancy, sex ratio and low maternal mortality stand positively the highest in the country, comparable to the standards of developed nations. But the social status of women, especially among the SC categories, does not often coincided with these indicators. Moreover, the SC women, compared to the women from the higher castes, undertake far larger socio-economic and familial responsibilities. Hopefully, this situation found a paradigm shift with the introduction of democratic decentralisation that serves as an instrument of development from bottom. In this context, the present study analyses the position and socio-political and economic empowerment of SC women in the context of democratic decentralisation through PRIs.

Significance of the Study

The rationale behind democratic decentralisation lays in the mass participation in local socio-political and economic affairs affecting the local people, particularly, the SC women and thus helps them to attain socio-political and economic base. In this context, democratic decentralisation forms an opportunity structure for SC women to come to the mainstream of the society. The supportive systems of democratic decentralisation such as Gramasabha, Self Help Groups, and Neighbourhood Groups play a major role in the empowerment of local population especially SC women.

The study focuses on the various aspects and dimensions of empowerment in general and of SC women in particular. For women, empowerment is the restructuring of gender relations within the family and the society at large. Women become empowered through collective reflections and decision making. Empowerment implies a fundamental redistribution of powers, which also allow women to renegotiate their existence on equitable basis. The researcher has reviewed many studies about SC, but most of them have not gone deep into the issues of decentralisation and empowerment of SC women. Besides being not up to date, they also are limited in their geographical and thematic coverage. The present study will thus be a welcome addition to the branch of gender studies and may also help the policy formulators to make changes in this direction.

Objectives

The primary objective of the study is to assess the socio-economic and political empowerment of SC women after the introduction of democratic decentralisation.

Specific objectives:

1. To study the specific and general schemes envisaged in the democratic decentralisation process for the empowerment of SC women.
2. To examine the implementation level of various schemes intended for the empowerment of SC women at various stages of democratic decentralisation.
3. To examine the awareness level of SC women about the various schemes in democratic decentralisation process for the empowerment of SC women.
4. To study the social empowerment of SC women.
5. To analyse the political and economic empowerment of the SC women after the implementation of democratic decentralisation.
6. To study the factors which hinder the empowerment of SC women in the democratic decentralisation process.

Hypotheses

1. Considerable size of the SC women is not aware of the various schemes envisaged for their development.
2. Decentralisation process does not lead to the social empowerment of SC women.
3. Decentralisation process may pave the way for the political and economic empowerment of these women.
4. There are many constraints which hinder the empowerment of the SC women in the democratic decentralisation process.

Definition of Major Concepts

Decentralisation

Decentralisation implies transfer of authority and responsibility from the central government to the district and subordinate levels to make development more locally sensitive and participatory. It involves a two dimensional process: (a) that increases the sensitivity of bureaucracy to local conditions and needs; and (b) wherein communities can participate in decision making on their local requirements and priorities in a more direct and immediate manner based on a system of leadership accountability and transparent information. It is, thus, obvious that decentralisation is expected to usher in more effective provision of local services.

Democratic Decentralisation

Democratic decentralisation is a process by which decentralisation is practiced through more democratic participation. It is indispensable to make the administration more democratic and to ensure people's participation in development programmes. It is an essential means to generate in the people the feeling that they have a right to participate in the government and that the development schemes provided in the country are for them too.

Participatory Planning

Participatory planning denotes people's involvement from initiation to the completion of plan. It is an advisable concept as it encompasses people's participation in decision –making, implementation of the decision, sharing of the benefits and evaluation. Under this process people are mobilized through local bodies in all stages of development planning from formation to implementation.

Dalits

The word Dalit is of relatively recent origin during the 1960s in public discourse. Marathi-speaking literary writers and neo-Buddhists by persuasion began to use the word Dalit in their literary works instead of Harijan or *achchuta*. Dalit writers who have popularized the word have expressed their notion of Dalit identity in their essays, poems, dramas, autobiographies, novels and short stories.

The word gained currency in public spheres during the SC-caste Hindu riots in Bombay in the early 1970s. Dalit Panthers, an activist group among the SCs, used the term to assert their identity for rights and self-respect. Later, the term has been used with a wider connotation. It includes all the oppressed and exploited sections of society. It has essentially emerged as a socio-political category.

Dalits are the poor and downtrodden. Generally, Dalit includes those termed in administrative parlance as SCs, STs, and OBCs. However, in day-to-day usage in political discourse, the term is so far mainly confined to Scheduled Castes.

Scheduled Castes

Caste in Sociology "are treated as an extreme form of social stratification characterized by fixed birth status, social discrimination and complete absence of vertical mobility for individuals"(Prakash, Sen 1980).

The Scheduled Caste is a term very commonly used in our day-to-day life but it is a political-legal term. The Simon Commission and subsequently the Government of India Act of 1935 first coined it. When India became independent this term was adopted in the constitution.

The term Scheduled Castes signifies those groups of people who were out of the caste system or the Varna hierarchy in the past. They comprise the bulk of untouchables. The untouchables were considered to be inferior because of their birth in particular caste.

Women Empowerment

Empowerment is a concept which crosscuts many disciplines and arenas. This is the process of increasing personal, interpersonal or political power through which individuals, families and communities can take action to improve their situations.

Braye and Preston, Shoot (1995) define empowerment has been defined in terms of:

1. Extending one's ability to take effective decisions.
2. Individuals and groups taking control of their circumstances and achieving their own goals, thereby being able to work towards maximizing the quality of their lives.
3. Enabling people who are disempowered to have more control over their lives, to have a greater voice in institutions, service and situations which affect them, and to exercise power over someone else rather than simply being the recipient of exercised power, helping people to regain their own power.

At the core of the concept of empowerment is the idea of power. Consequently, empowerment can be viewed as encompassing:

1. Psychological power having the personal confidence, self-esteem and motivation to initiate change;
2. Social power having the resources of information, skills and general knowhow to initiate change; and
3. Political power having the capacity to effectively engage in decision-making processes and participating in collective decision-making.

Operational Definition

Empowerment is operationally defined for the purpose of the present study as a process by which Scheduled Caste women improve their access and capacity to make effective choices in their social, economic and political life through participation in the grassroots institutions such as SHGs, NHGs and Gramasabhas.

Theoretical Framework

Power Theory – Jo Rowlands

Jo Rowlands' (Reference) contextual interdisciplinary and multidimensional theory visualizes empowerment as a process of transition from a state of powerlessness to a state of relative control over one's life, destiny, and environment. This transition can manifest itself in an improvement in the perceived as well as the actual ability of individuals to control.

The analysis of the case of Honduras by Rowlands (1997) shows that the empowerment process will take a form which arises out of a particular ethnic historical, economic, geographic, political and social location; out of specific life experience and out of the interaction of the above with gender relations prevailing in society.

The power to be obtained according to Rowlands falls into three categories:

- *Power with*: Organization, Group action, Functioning
- *Power to*: Involving in income-generation programme, Employment Productive force, Create new possibilities, Control over income
- *Power over*: Involving community, Political-Activity, Controlling Compliance, Resistance, Awareness, and Access.

For *Keller and Mbewe* (Reference) empowerment is "a process whereby women become organized themselves to increase their own self-reliance, to assert their independent right, to make choices and to control resource which will assist in challenging and eliminating their lifelong 'subordination'". In this sense women's movement for empowerment challenges the existing patriarchic bureaucracy.

Amartya Sen (Reference) - Development as Freedom

Freedom to attain self-sufficiency on basic fulfillment is most often curbed and limited by poverty. Amartya Sen's theoretical framework confirms that economic poverty, in the form of low income, limits the basic fulfillments like eating adequately, securing comfortable clothing and shelter. Poverty also enhances gender inequality in an unimaginable way especially in the areas of labour force participation and literacy. Hence emphasis should be laid on promoting women's agencies. Due to lack of access to economic resources there is a whooping low degree of participation of women in day-to-day economic affairs. However, there is plenty of evidence available to prove that women can seize chances, take control of their social arrangements, depart/deviate from the standard practice of male ownership and take economic initiatives with much more success, better than their counterparts. Their active participation helps not only to generate income but also provides the social benefits which come from their enhanced social status and economic independence. Thus, their participation has two implications; their self improvement and social change in general. According to Sen, Social development is inhibited by poverty, and development on such areas should focus on man's capacity to achieve different valuable human functions. Sen stresses the point that men are not rational fools to be motivated only by self interested economic activities of production and exchange, but should be motivated equally by other values like justice, fairness, trust, honoring of contracts and civil duties. Sedn cites cases of micro credit programmes which bring about major changes in society. According to him 'Capacity Approach' serves as a guide for a just world with less inequalities combined with all micro policies with macro democratic governance structure for enhancing human capabilities. Such Capability Approach can be used to analyse how and the extent to which the democratic institutions can increase the capabilities of women.

Naila Kabeer - UNRISD

Empowering women is both a process as well as an outcome. Naila Kabeer (Reference) has discussed this issue and gives her outline of the empowerment process.

Resources ⟶ Agency ⟶ Achievements
(Preconditions) (Process) (Outcomes)

It can be measured as an outcome against expected accomplishments. According to her this process is entitled to initiate change at all levels - individual, their inner sense of self, their access to material resources, among ones relationship within the family or household or it can alter the position in the wider hierarchies of the economy and state. She argues that grass root level participation is mandatory to control resources, determine agendas and make decisions.

Resources may include all material and various human and social resources which will enhance the ability to exercise choices. These resources can be acquired through a variety of social relationships pertaining to various institutional domains like society, family, market, state and community.

Process, in the model, refers to the ability to define one's goals and efforts towards achieving them. The role of agency is emphasized here. Agency is an observable action which encompasses individuals to their activity. Agency is otherwise operationalized as 'decision- making' which manifests in the actions of bargaining, negotiation, deceiving and manipulating, supervising, resisting and other cognitive processes of reflection and analysis. These can be exercised either by an individual or by an organization or formal or informal groups. This theoretical framework helps to analyse whether the SHGs and Gramasabhas play the role of strong agency in the women empowerment process.

Lucy Lazo

According to Lucy (Reference), empowerment centers around an adult women for two reasons; first, for their adult lives have given them much exposure to varied experiences of subordination which will help to focus their problems very well. Second, the transformation of these women is fundamental to break the intergenerational reproduction of patriarchal authority. Participation of women in small groups like SHGs with a collective agenda of understanding of domination, organization and mobilization and setting up of a wider political agenda which will lead to a new collective arrangement and transformed citizenship at the macro level is vial in their empowerment. This will in turn render a greater sense of freedom and personal competence; reshape motherhood values and renegotiation of domestic relationships. This theoretical framework will help to analyse the phases of empowerment of women venturing in micro enterprises.

Michael Foucault (Reference)

Foucault focuses on localized forms of resistance at micro level with respect to the construction of power within day-to–day interactions. His ideology of power explains how the micro credit compartmentalizes women from top to bottom. His theory illustrates the linkages between macro and micro dimensions of power and highlights the structure of gender and class inequalities and more importantly how women struggle to resist such inequalities. Micro credit can be analyzed through the concept of discipline of power which highlights the mechanisms of inclusion and exclusion that at a given time becomes politically, economically and socially useful. It also offers the ways to understand the concept of resistance. Foucault compares power to the two poles of human body; the first pole works through 'anatomo-politics of the human body which aims to increase docility, whereas the second pole, 'bio-politics of the human body' works through a series of regulatory controls. According to him 'bio- politics' allows governments to view its population as resources rather than mere citizens. At micro level, mechanisms like SHGs work through the credit guidelines which increases the money making capability of women, whereas at macro level it works through lending policies and excludes or includes certain groups of the population at specific period in the development process. This theory will help to get a clear picture of regulatory and disciplinary nature of micro credit managed by SHGs and Gramasabhas and probe whether repayment of loans and managing the enterprises are becoming burden to women by making them more submissive rather than empowered.

Research Design

In order to understand the nature and process of empowerment among SC women, a descriptive analysis of the present situation is made. The descriptive research design is used for the present study as it tries to describe the social, political and economic empowerment of SC women and the hindrances faced in the process of empowerment. As it is a systematic and scientific study, the results obtained can be treated as a sign post for further studies in the similar direction.

Pilot Study

A pilot study was conducted among a few households to ensure the feasibility of the study and availability of data. It was conducted with the objectives: (1) to obtain preliminary information about the universe, i.e., about various groups in SC women, and the social, political and the economic barriers they faced; and (2) to examine the scope for conducting a research study on the empowerment of SC women.

Universe

SC women in Kerala formed the universe of the study. Since there are many divisions within the Dalit community, it was decided to include only the Scheduled Caste women from the sample areas selected for the study. The unit of study is each Scheduled Caste woman in Kerala participating in any of the developmental programmes of PRIs such as SHGs, NHGs and Gramasabha.

Sampling Method

The field of the study was Palakkad and Thiruvananthapuram districts in Kerala. 300 SC women from both the districts were selected for the purpose of the study. Multistage random sampling and purposive sampling were used for identifying the sample. A 4 stages procedure was used for the selection of wards.

Step 1- Selection of Districts: Two districts with the highest share of SC population in the state were selected. These districts namely Palakkad and Thiruvananthapuram jointly account for 25.7 per cent of the SC population in the state (Table 2.1).

Table 2.1: Percentage and share of SC population in Kerala, 2001

Sl. No.	Districts	Percent of SC population	Share of the State
(1)	(2)	(3)	(4)
1.	Thiruvananthapuram	11.5	11.9
2.	Kollam	12.5	10.3
3.	Pathanamthitta	13.2	5.2
4.	Alappuzha	9.5	6.4
5.	Kottayam	7.7	4.8
6.	Idukki	14.1	5.1
7.	Eranakulam	8.5	8.4

(Table Contd...)

(1)	(2)	(3)	(4)
8.	Trissur	11.9	11.3
9.	Palakkad	16.5	13.8
10.	Malappuram	7.9	9.1
11.	Kozhikode	7.0	6.4
12.	Wayanad	4.2	1.1
13.	Kannur	4.1	2.9
14.	Kasaragod	7.5	100.0
	Kerala	9.0	

Source of Data: Government of Kerala (2001)

Step 2 Selection of Panchayat: Based on the proportion of SC population to the total population ten Panchayats each were selected from both the districts. (Tables 2.2 and 2.3)

Table 2.2: Name of selected Panchayats in Palakkad district, 2001

Sl. No.	Name of Panchayat	No. of Households	Population	SC Population	% of SC Population
1.	Peringottukurissi	4963	23234	8493	36.6
2.	Kottai	4360	20992	6911	32.9
3.	Keralassery	3202	14755	4682	31.7
4.	Kongad	5736	27792	8507	30.6
5.	Pookkottukavu	3005	13614	3957	29.1
6.	Thenkurissi	5643	26674	7411	27.8
7.	Peruvemba	3806	18433	4790	26.0
8.	Chalavara	4091	21042	5423	25.8
9.	Mankara	3591	17669	4389	24.8
10.	Vaniamkulam	6360	29496	7235	24.5

Source of Data: Census of Kerala, 2001

Table 2.3: Name of selected Panchayats in Thiruvanathapuram district, 2001

Sl. No.	Name of Panchayat	No. of Households	Population	SC Population	% of SC Population
1.	Cherunniyoor	4069	17918	4406	24.6
2.	Chemmaruthy	7057	30918	7002	22.6
3.	Mudakkal	8144	34416	7135	20.7
4.	Pazhayakunnummel	6091	25007	5090	20.4
5.	Azhoor	6439	28831	5535	19.2
6.	Kizhuvalam	7294	32728	6270	19.2
7.	Mangalapuram	7720	34692	6574	18.9
8.	Venganoor	8205	33372	6203	18.6
9.	Nagaroor	6349	26696	4801	18.0
10.	Kilimanoor	4881	20055	3581	17.9

Source of Data: Census of Kerala, 2001

Step 3 - Selection of households: From each selected Panchayat, one ward having the highest percentage of SC women has been selected. The selected wards for the present study are given in table 2.4.

Table 2.4: Name of Wards selected for the present study

Palakkad			Thiruvananthapuram		
Sl.No.	Name of Panchayat	Ward No.	Sl.No.	Name of Panchayat	Ward No.
1.	Peringottukurissi	2	1.	Cherunniyoor	8
2.	Kottai	11	2.	Chemmaruthy	3
3.	Keralassery	4	3.	Mudakkal	15
4.	Kongad	11	4.	Pazhayakunnummel	6
5.	Pookkottukavu	3	5.	Azhoor	1
6.	Thenkurissi	7	6.	Kizhuvalam	6
7.	Peruvemba	3	7.	Mangalapuram	13
8.	Chalavara	9	8.	Venganoor	1
9.	Mankara	6	9.	Nagaroor	13
10.	Vaniamkulam	6	10.	Kilimanoor	3

From each ward, 15 SC households were selected using purposive sampling method. Purposive sampling was used since the researcher wanted to purposefully select those households having women participating in SHGs, Gramasabha and NHGs. Thus the total number of households selected for the present study is 300. One woman from each house who is actively participating in women empowerment programmes was interviewed.

Tools for Data Collection

The major tool for collecting primary data was a structured interview schedule. The schedule contained a total of one hundred and one questions comprising of both open ended and closed end questions. The schedule was structured and administered in such a way as to get data regarding awareness level, social empowerment, economic empowerment, political empowerment and constraints. Observation was another method used for collecting primary data.

Pre-test

The reliability and validity of the interview schedule was tested through a pre-test of the interview schedule done on 40 participants of SHGs, NHGs and Gramasabha in Idukki district in Kerala State. Pre-test revealed that certain question were more relevant. Repetitions were avoided and confusing questions were suitably modified. The questions were then finalized.

Variables

The variables used in the study were age (age is related to performance level), marital status (it is linked to facing of different challenges), income (shows the level of financial autonomy), place of residence (mobility aspects are related to this variable), type of family (helps in the analysis of role in decision making processes) and group membership (useful while analyzing group dynamics). The independent and dependent variables were found out and their interrelations were established in this study.

Analysis of Data

The collected data was processed with the help of SPSS software and necessary statistical analysis was made. The major statistical techniques used in the study are Chi square test and one way ANOVA. The functioning of SHGs, NHGs and Gramasabha were analysed descriptively using percentage as well as cross tabular method. The awareness level about various programmes were analysed with the help of Chi square test. Empowerment of SC women in the social, economic and political domains were analysed with selected indicators. They were cross tabulated with significant independent variables to understand the varying perceptions among the various categories of the studied population. The data was further analysed with the statistical techniques such as Chi-square and one way ANOVA.

Scheme of Chapterisation

The first chapter introduces the problem and outlines the review of the relevant literature. The methodology is discussed in the second chapter.

The third chapter on awareness level and empowerment of SC women describes the awareness level of SC women, about the developmental opportunities as well as the choices made by them in the process of development.

The fourth chapter titled social empowerment of SC women analyses the expansion of the social context of SC women through the participation in various schemes. It also measures the social empowerment of the population under study.

The fifth chapter analyses the economic empowerment of SC women and the consequent empowerment levels in different realms and the sixth chapter examines the expansion of political empowerment of SC women.

Seventh chapter picturizes the constraints in the empowerment of SC women. The last, i.e. eighth chapter summaries the findings and outline the conclusions and suggestions.

Limitations of the Study

While this research work constitutes an important study of Kerala Scheduled Caste women, there are some limitations which are quite natural in a study of this kind. This study is based on two districts in Kerala which is a limitation in understanding empowerment on Scheduled Caste women.

Similarly, sample has been drawn only from participants in the grassroots institutions like SHGs, NHGs and Gramasabaha.

3

Awareness Level and Empowerment of Scheduled Caste Women

Any society is more concerned with the level of awareness, since it is largely the factor that becomes decisive in explaining the readiness with which the persons concerned to participate, at some level or other, in the various developmental activities. The factor of awareness is much more than a mere feeling, or inclination. These feelings of awareness are more transitory and are likely to be easily influenced by several factors. On the other hand, the factor of awareness is fairly enduring within a specific social context. It becomes effective in a social context as it is only within social structures that awareness gets reinforced through stable interpersonal relationships. It must be borne in mind that the awareness is a factor in social reality with which the individuals are related. Thus, awareness is built up through specific process in which the individuals themselves play a determinant role. Hence awareness is not a mere attribute of an individual, but demands an active role on the part of the individual in its crystallization. This is the reason why one often speaks of social awareness, thus implying that awareness is a product. Awareness in any specific form enables an individual to seek information about certain aspect of social reality through varied sources. It may be through other persons like local leaders, developmental officials, elders or mass media.

The present chapter refers to context of decentralized planning process for the development of SC people. Under the scheme of Panchayat Raj Institutions, Gramasabha is the most prominent body as if is visualized as the platform for people to interact with their representatives and officials and to take decisions relating to their development. The Gramasabha as a collective body discusses the issues and problems, needs and aspirations of the village, as well as problems faced by special groups. Gramasabha is the center of democracy at village level and ensures participative democracy; it is not only an institution articulating the needs and aspirations of the community but also a forum for mobilizing community participation. Gramasabhas were constitutionally recognized in 1992. The 73rd Constitutional Amendment strengthened grassroots democracy, by bringing local governance closer to the people, particularly the marginalized communities. Strong grassroots democracy presupposes *inter alia* enlightened, responsible, public-spirited citizenry, who ensure qualitatively and quantitatively enhanced and inclusive people's participation, transparency in local governance, accountability, responsiveness, popular control, high quality of leadership and decision making in lower ranks of Local Self Government Institutions. These fundamental features of grass-root democracy are directly depend on people's awareness about the structures, processes, profiles and features of the institutions created to facilitate democratization, especially the Gramasabhas that allows citizens to participate directly. People's knowledge about the powers, functions, rights and responsibilities of Gramasabhas is one of the basic determining factors in the process of democratic decentralization. Awareness leads to awakening; awaking leads to change. "Knowledge has increasingly become a major source of power and control" (Tandon, 2002).

"While knowledge is passive, awareness is active" Mere knowledge, however, it is not enough to promote democracy and to busy about consequent social change or economic developments. It is one's knowledge that stimulates active citizen involvement and commitment to the common concerns. Knowledge becomes power only when it changes the existing situations of individual institutions, circumstances, attitudes and behaviour. Awareness is the result of conscientisation, though without knowledge it is not possible. In this sense, awareness goes beyond the dictionary meaning. It is with this understanding that the concept of knowledge and awareness are used interchangeably in this chapter.

Awareness of an issue or situation is a precondition for active participation. It generates relevant questions, comments, critical intrusions, constructive suggestions, and crucial involvements in problem solving. "Participation is a process by which stakeholder's influence and share control over priority setting, policymaking, resource allocations, or program implementation" (Klugman, Jeny 2002). "Political participation enlarges the minds of individuals, familiarizes them with interests, which lie beyond the immediacy of personal circumstances and environment, and encourages them to acknowledge that public concerns are the proper one to which they should pay attention"(Oldfeild,1990). This participation is a crucial factor in the empowering process. Thandon writes, although "Knowledge is not only a source of power and control in contemporary society, but it is through knowledge, participation and empowerment is facilitated" (Thandon, 2002). People's participation is the necessary condition for a vibrant grass roots democracy. Awareness generates participation. Awareness is very often considered one of the determinants of participation in the context of decentralization process (Sethi, S 2006)

However, scholars like Oldfeild argue that participation especially political participation creates awareness and familiarity, making it a precondition for informed and involved citizenship (Oldfeild, 1990). Nevertheless, both awareness and participation are inextricably linked to citizenship and democratic decentralization. Guess that awareness leads to participation, and participation leads to awareness. One sees a virtuous cycle.

In Kerala, during the People's Plan Campaign (PPC) and the Left Democratic Front (LDF) Government carried out a massive campaign, which focused on attracting people to the Grama Sabhas as well as the planning process. But in Kerala, planning has also been made as an instrument for social mobilization in support of decentralization. The mass mobilization was intended to ensure that correct decisions were made at the local level, to bring about certain change of attitude among the participants and to make up mass pressure from below for democratic reforms. The people's Campaign actively seeks to nurture a civic culture that will strengthen grass root democratic institutions. A radical transformation of the development culture of the state is a necessary prerequisite for successful participatory decentralization". (Isaac *et al* 2000).

However, awareness building in specific terms on the power, functions, rights and responsibilities of Gramasabhas were not effectively carried out during the campaign. The PPC was, indeed, a successful political campaign, but not an effective awareness campaign. Thus the spirits were raised, but the contents forgotten. Moreover, the campaign did not give much priority to the marginalized populations and the geographical margins, where the poor people lived and worked. In the media centered mass mobilization process, members of various technical and other committees, the elite, middle class and lower middle class sections got involved, It was unfortunate to note that the poorest people did not participate in the Gramasabhas due to the lack of awareness, and they participated only with the view of grabbing physical benefits. The quality of participation declined due to lack of awareness of the constitutional process among these sections (Issac, 2000). The 73rd constitutional and Kerala Panchayat Raj Act (KPRA) presupposes the citizens know any about the powers, functions and responsibilities of Grama Sabhas as the people's platform form direct democracy.

The Central and State governments in India have a number of plans and programmes for economic and social development of the SC population. Over the last fifty years, many different interventions and strategies have been formulated by the government and the non-government agencies to develop the condition of women in India. Large number of Self Help Groups (SHGs) and Neighbourhood Groups (NHGs) were started in various parts of the country for the purpose of empowering the women. A number of SHGs and NHGs have been introduced in the state of Kerala for the women empowerment programme and on 1st April of 1999 a new form of NHG was launched in the form of *Kudumbashree* project. Kudumbasree is a poverty eradication project launched by the Government of Kerala, with support of the NABARD, for eradicating absolute poverty, in particular among women, within a decade.

The SHGs have played a catalytic role in bringing the participation of women in development process in the country. Now a large section of women in India, individually and collectively, are contributing to the development of the country through credit, savings, small income generating activities, training in skills, health, family planning, literacy and legal rights. The SHGs, NHGs, and CDS, particularly the Kudumbasree, have made perceptible changes in the lives of women in Kerala. The present study probes into the performance of women groups, particularly the SHGs and NHGs, and Gramasabhas as agents of women empowerment in Kerala.

SHGs are generally found to be very effective in improving the knowledge and skill of the rural folk through informal education and training programmes. Its success depended on the type of training, number of training sessions attended and also the quality of training. The Community Organizers and Co-ordinators got trained at the apex level. Classes and discussions were organised by resource persons, officials and banks directly to SHG members at the community level and this have helped to raise their levels of information, awareness, and knowledge.

The initial condition towards any empowerment include participation by the individuals to raise their awareness about the structure and function of grassroots bodies, the levels of government, system of governance and so on. Another disappointing observation made was the poor awareness level among the SC women. The overall awareness with regard to Panchayat Raj set up; among the respondents was very poor miserably poor was awareness in regard to other levels of the government. Most of them failed to explain the function or role of a ward member. It was surprising to find poor awareness with regard to the constitutional grass roots bodies, like Gramasabha. For that matter, their knowledge was either partial or very little even with regard to the Grama Panchayat of which they were members. Most of the respondents could only point out one or two civic functions being looked after by the Panchayat, and nothing more.

Other than the Panchayat Raj bodies, the awareness level among the SC women respondents about the rural development programmes, other governmental functionaries and their supportive mechanism like NGO organs was not contrary to expectations. A very few among them had some faint idea about the on-going rural development programmes, nature of urban local bodies and the broader set up of officials at village, block or higher levels.

In the area of social transformation and liberation, government supportive agencies play a significant role in the process of women's empowerment. It is an eye-opener for millions of women who are in a position to understand and to have a discussion or dialogue through interactions. Women's organizations are acting as intermediaries to rural (Local) women to empower them psychologically. This enables them to get rid of many barriers for socially and both psychologically.

Profile of the Respondents

The scheduled castes women constitute the downtrodden categories, in our society. These women struggle a lot so that they do not lead their life in a good way. Their opportunities were often poor. These SC women live in thatched houses (huts) in congested manner. They work hard to earn and live. The SC women have to depend on their husband most of, who are drunkards, who never give any money to their wives. These women play a dual role to feed their children, educate them and to provide them safety and security. These women never take care of their health and they are more eager to look after their kids and husbands' health.

The normal upbringing of a girl in the rural society is directed towards marriage as soon as she reaches maturity. This implies the early takeover of family responsibility. Women in the rural household were counted upon no less to contribute an additional helping hand both at home and at the land. Their formal education is not considered to be important.

Circumstances were that women had to toil all day long that she was not able to know what is happening in and around her. She leads a very prejudistic life. Not busy aware of anything in this world, she is not able to participate or avail any programmes that are implemented for her welfare. The interview was conducted with 300 respondents and out of them (31%) came under the age groups of 26-33; 27.3 per cent come under the age group of 34-41, 25.3 percent of the respondents belong to the age group of 42 and above and the remaining 16.3 per cent of respondents belongs to the age category of 18-25.

These respondents were classified with reference to their attainment of education. (59.7%) attained their education only up to primary level. 56 respondents (18.7%) were illiterate, 44 respondents had education up to pre-degree and 21 respondents (7%) were graduates. In this study 271 respondents were married. 4 per cent were unmarried, 9 respondents were deserted by their husbands and 8 respondents were divorced. This variable is not significant because 271 respondents were married. This happens because the SC women were married in their tender age itself. 130 (45%) respondents got married at the age of 18-21, 111 (38.5%) were married at the age of 22 and above and the remaining 47 women (16.3%) were married below 18 years.

The economic status of the SC women respondents were considered in the study. The respondents in the study were identified with the ration card, which they have. But the respondents were exploited by this process. The ration card divides the people's economic status as Above Poverty Line (APL) and Below Poverty Line (BPL). 165 respondents (55%) were BPL and 131 respondents (43.7 %) were APL. But many of the respondents were wrongly included in the APL category. They were exploited by the political parties known by different names and the remaining 4 respondents out of 300 did not even posses ration cards. This fact was further analysed with the significant independent variables as follows.

Awareness

"Teach a man, teach an individual, teach a woman, teach a family", if families are educated, then the society also gets educated as families make the society". So this education of a woman should be the top priority of all government policies. Deprivation of knowledge or education to women will be a stumbling block to all reformation. Thus, the corner stone of the strategy to help women empower themselves is to facilitate various processes of action through which awareness can be generated. This awareness if created will definitely stir their innate desire to know more things and motivate them towards the desired goal. The role of SHGs lies in creating awareness among women with regard to education, sanitation, account-keeping, savings, availing credit, prompt repayment, subsides, etc.

Information is indispensable for the functioning of true governments developmental agencies. The greater the access of the citizen to information, the greater would be the responsiveness of the government to community needs. Without proper information, people cannot adequately exercise their rights and responsibilities as citizens or make informal choices. The knowledge should be the value of right to awareness as a critical factor in socio-cultural, economic and political development is being increasingly felt. It is also to strengthen the idea of participatory democracy for without information, one cannot possibly make informed has attracted the attention of policy makers, political thinkers and socio-economic approach to development via special policies like National Commission for Women 1993, National Policy for the empowerment of women 2001, Reservation of seats in the local bodies of Panchayats etc. However, it is believed that there still exists a wide gender gap leading one to question the success of these efforts as it did not turn out to be a real success at the grass roots level due to the lack of awareness among the SC women regarding the functions of government agencies. The table 3.1 shows that, 41.3 per cent of women have awareness to a great extent about the functions of government agencies, while 52.3 per cent of women have awareness only to some extent. 6.3 per cent of women do not have any awareness about these agencies at all. This fact was further analysed with the significant independent variables as follows the awareness about the function of government agencies by age wise.

Age and Awareness

The ability and willingness to participate in agencies of women may be significant by related to the age group. In fact collective empowerment comes by awareness capacity. The role of age groups and generations has been of considerable interest to sociologists. So age been taken as an important variable in this study. The analysis of data was undertaken on the basis of the respondents as shown below. Awareness was further analysed with regard to significant independent variables.

Table 3.1: Awareness about the function of government agencies by age wise

Age	Awareness about the Function of Govt. Agencies			Total	χ^2	df	p-value
	To a Great Extent (%)	To some Extent (%)	Not at all (%)				
18-25	26 (53.1)	23 (46.9)	–	49	71.239**	6	0.005
26-33	54 (58.1)	22 (23.7)	17 (18.3)	93			
34-41	21(25.6)	59 (72.0)	2 (2.4)	82			
42 Above	23 (30.3)	53 (69.7)	–	76			
Total	124 (41.3)	157 (52.3)	19 (6.3)	300			

** Significant at 1% level ($p<0.01$)

Age is an important demographic variable that can influence the level of awareness as the experiences and perception of different age groups vary according to the social context of their living. The cross table analysis between the variables like age and the awareness regarding government agencies was found to be statistically significant is given in the Chi- square value was significance level. It was noted that 58.1 per cent of the respondents in the age group of 26-33, had a great level of awareness with respect to the functions of SHGs, NHGs and Gramasabha.

The table also indicates that, the level of awareness was found to be moderate. Among, the higher age groups i.e.; the 34-41 and 42 and above age groups, 72 per cent and 69.7 per cent respectively expressed moderate level of awareness. Briefly we can infer from the analysis that among the younger age group enjoyed a high level of awareness while, among the elder groups, were found to be moderate.

Education and Awareness

State provides education to its subjects, in order to improve their living standards and ideology. For the purpose of the study education was analysed with reference to awareness about different government mechanism.

Education is one of the basic institutions of any society. It is one among the various means by which members of the society are socialized to become aware of their social situation. One of the main purposes of education in a civilized society is, to help people learn to access information, to make wise decision and choices and to make them aware of their needs and requirements. Lack of communication, results in absence of information and education, which in turn results in backwardness of the area. Social campaigning might be considered as a major tool by means of awareness building, like raising education, experience and action in the area. The projects used both these viz. social campaigning and village level meetings effectively and raised the level of awareness in women regarding the various schemes and benefits are available. (Jayesh Talati and V. Venkatakrishnan, 2001).

Table 3.2: Education and awareness about the function of government agencies

Education	Awareness about the Function of Govt. Agencies				χ^2	df	p-value
	To a Great Extent (%)	To some Extent (%)	Not at all (%)	Total			
Illiterate	11(19.6)	43 (76.8)	2 (3.6)	56	60.030**	6	0.005
Primary	63 (35.2)	99 (55.3)	17 (9.5)	179			
Pre-degree	29 (65.9)	15 (34.1)	–	44			
Graduate	21 (100)	–	–	21			
Total	124 (41.3)	157 (52.3)	19 (6.3)	300			

** Significant at 1% level ($p<0.01$)

The table reveals that the relationship between educational attainment and awareness is quite significant. It indicated that higher the educational attainment of the respondents, the higher their awareness respectively. In the above table it is observed that the two categories Graduate and Pre-degree with higher educational attainment showed positive awareness, i.e., 100 per cent and 65.9 per cent respectively demonstrated a higher degree of awareness. Thus the relationship between educational attainment and awareness is significant as far as graduates and respondents with pre-degree are concerned. This proves that education provides not only new avenues of opportunity and learning but also knowledge about different agencies necessary for their upliftment. At the same time, illiterate women had very poor knowledge about the women's development agencies, reflecting their poor knowledge of various developmental programmes too. Those with highest percentages of awareness were the highly educated. Consequently, it is inferred that higher the educational attainment, higher would be their level of awareness.

The calculated χ^2 value for 6 degrees of freedom was found to be 60.030, for a corresponding p-value of 0.005. Hence, the null hypothesis is rejected. Where there is a strong relationship between the education of the respondents and their awareness level about the functioning of the government agencies.

Age at Marriage and Awareness

The researcher's next attempt was to examine the dissemination of awareness among the SC women at various age groups. It was found that the awareness is high among the middle age group than others. This is because higher the age group, greater would be the experience. Overall, the middle age will have more space to interact with their counterparts. This may also indicate that with the increase in literacy levels over the years, the publicity through the newspapers, social workers, local politicians, NGOs and SHGs led to creation of a higher level of awareness among the SC women, especially in the relatively middle age group.

The age of marriage of SC women is also one of the important factors as far as awareness level is concerned. Majority of SC women were found to be married at a lower age. Therefore, they were bound to be burdened by many more family responsibilities at a very young age itself. Since they bore the burden on their shoulders, they had to work in order to earn money. To earn money, she must be aware of all possible ways. Here the data is analysed on the basis of their age at marriage and their awareness level in the table below.

Table 3.3: Age at marriage and awareness about the function of government agencies

Age at Marriage	Awareness about the Function of Govt. Agencies				χ^2	df	p-value
	To Great Extent (%)	To some Extent (%)	Not at all (%)	Total			
Below 18 years	10(21.3)	37(78.7)	–	47			
18-21	51(39.2)	66(50.8)	13(10)	130	31.618**	4	0.005
22 above	60(54.1)	51(45.9)	–	111			
Total	121(42)	154(53.5)	13(13)	288			

** Significant at 1% level (p<0.01)

It is obvious from the table 3.3 that 54.1 per cent of the respondents who were married at the age of 22 and above are better aware about the functioning of women development agencies. Another notable point is that below 18 years category, 78.7 per cent of respondents had only moderate knowledge. Moreover, on this category women were married quite early. Hence they were more interested in SHGs than Gramasabhas. The others, in the same age group were also very much interested in the activities of SHGs and NHGs because their agencies conducted meetings in their houses (one among them) on a weekly basis. They could easily make it to the meeting. Besides this 39.2 per cent of respondents belonging to the age group (18-21) engaged themselves actively in the organizations.

The calculated χ^2 value for 4 degrees of freedom was 31.618, for a corresponding p-value of 0.005. Hence, the null hypothesis is rejected. It can be conclude that, there is indeed a strong relationship between the age of the respondents at marriage and their awareness level about the functioning of the government agencies.

Monthly Income and Awareness

It is largely found that SC women are often unable to access the governmental information, because of their poor income, they always involved in the seasonal occupation to meet their livelihood. This presents them with better opportunity to study government programs. Income levels and earning capacity is one of the important factors that helps to acquire knowledge. It is visible that, income and awareness have a close association. Moreover, higher income group have easy access with the government agencies owing to the influence of mass media like T.V, News paper etc, which amount to easily enrich their knowledge.

Table 3.4: Monthly income and awareness about the function of government agencies

Monthly Income (Rs.)	Awareness about the function of Govt. Agencies				χ^2	df	p-value
	To Great Extent (%)	To some Extent (%)	Not at all (%)	Total			
501-1000	54(34.2)	90(57.0)	14(8.9)	158	25.020**	4	0.005
1001-3000	42(39.6)	59(55.7)	5(4.7)	106			
30001 above	28(77.8)	8(22.2)	–	36			
Total	124(41.3)	157(52.3)	19(6.3)	300			

** Significant at 1% level ($p<0.01$)

Majority of the respondents were aware of the functions of women developmental agencies. Majority of respondents who belong to the income group of above Rs. 3000 claimed regular participation in Gramasabha, and they are very much familiar with the aims and benefits of it. They have also received more benefits through Grama Panchayat, because of decentralization. They do not have enough time to participate in Gramasabha meetings as they had tight work schedule. But they regularly attended the SHG and NHG meetings. Only a minority of the respondents acknowledged that they were not aware of the role and functions of governmental supportive systems. From these it may be assumed that there is an overall improvement in awareness of women with regard to Panchayat, SHGs and NHGs activities.

It was recognised that the main obstacles to SC women's empowerment is the low level of educational attainment and poverty. Keeping this in mind, the government of Kerala has framed various policies, designed specific interventions and implemented many programmes to eradicate poverty and to provide educational concession to the vulnerable sections of the society. The calculated χ^2 value for 4 degrees of freedom was 25.020; with a corresponding p-value of 0.005. Hence the null hypotheses are rejected and conclude that, there is a significant relationship between the respondent's monthly income and their awareness regarding the functioning of the government agencies.

Knowledge of Specific Programmes

The empowerment of SC women can be achieved through the knowledge of various developmental programmes. The Government of India and state agencies have implement numerous general schemes and specific programmes for the empowerment of SC women. The empowerment of the SC women through the specific programmes not only empowers the individual woman, but also has empowers the family and the community as a whole. Lack of knowledge of SC women with regard to government schemes clearly indicates the slow development of the community. It is believed that if the SC women had benefits from the government sponsored programmes, it would further pave the way for their advancement. The below table clearly indicates that about 52.7 percent of SC women had to a great extent of knowledge of specific programmes while 37.3 percent had knowledge "to some extent" about the same. It is worrisome to note that about 10 percent of the SC women have no knowledge about the specific programmes. This was subjected to further analysis (with the significant independent variables) as follows.

Education and knowledge of Specific Programmes

Education has distinct characteristics. An educated individual has more knowledge and awareness than the uneducated individual, such an individual is capable of or accessing information through the available medium. This knowledge provides a platform that would facilitate a discussion among the family members, thus widening the perception of the individual. Hence, an educated person, when compared to uneducated or less educated, may have better knowledge and favourable attitude towards various programmes.

Table 3.5: Education and knowledge of specific programmes

Education	Knowledge of specific programmes of SC Women			Total	χ^2	df	p-value
	To a Great Extent (%)	To Some Extent (%)	Not at all (%)				
Illiterate	13 (23.2)	30 (53.6)	13 (23.2)	56	42.298**	6	0.005
Primary	97 (54.2)	66 (36.9)	16 (8.9)	179			
Pre-degree	28 (63.6)	15 (34.1)	1 (2.3)	44			
Graduate	20 (95.2)	1 (4.8)	–	21			
Total	158 (52.7)	112 (37.3)	30 (10.0)	300			

** Significant at 1% level ($p<0.01$)

Even though the state and central governments had implemented many programmes to empower the SC women in the rural areas, only 4.8 per cent of the educated graduates were aware of those programmes to some extent. With respect to the illiterates 53.6 per cent claimed to be aware about the programmes to "some extent". But 23.2 per cent were not aware of any programmes in the Panchayat, meant to empower them. It may be concluded that lack of awareness hindered participation and subsequently any benefits. Hence, they were not empowered by the decentralizing process.

23.2 per cent of the illiterates were not aware of any measures, that the government put forth to develop them. Thus indicated that publicity was not effective; in other words developmental officers and mass media were not efficient. Some respondents came to know about these things from their friends and neighbours. The publicity could be made effective, if public meetings were organized regularly. The awareness should be concrete, if it is concrete, the SC women in the state will be empowered by all means. Their poverty will be alleviated, and they will be educated.

The same was analysed using the χ^2 test. The calculated χ^2 value for 6 degrees of freedom was 42.298 with its corresponding p-value is 0.005. Hence the null hypotheses are rejected and conclude that, there exist a strong relationship between the education of the respondents and their knowledge about specific programs.

Occupation and knowledge of Specific Programs

It is more important to identify the reach of the government programmes among the SC women. Moreover, it is important to study the reach of the implemented programmes and their benefits. Work place would also be a common platform for discussion and experience sharing.

Table 3.6: Occupation and knowledge of specific programmes

Occupation	Knowledge of specific programmes of SC Women			Total	χ^2	df	p-value
	Always (%)	To Some Extent (%)	Not at all (%)				
Employed	44 (81.5)	9 (16.7)	1 (1.9)	54	35.686**	6	0.005
Self employed	26 (56.5)	20 (43.5)	–	46			
Labour	48 (38.7)	55 (44.4)	21 (16.9)	124			
Unemployed	40 (52.6)	28 (36.8)	8 (10.5)	76			
Total	158 (52.7)	112 (37.3)	30 (10.0)	300			

** Significant at 1% level ($p<0.01$)

As many as 81.5 per cent of employed respondents were aware about the various development programmes for SC women, undertaken by Panchayat. They came to know about it from co-workers and usually discuss these welfare programmes implemented with their co-workers. It was found that the ignorance and unawareness of the unemployed respondents (10.5%) was due to the absence of a common working place to share the knowledge of these programmes. The developmental programmes have brought about a positive change in SC women's image. The study indicates that if the awareness level increases, their knowledge about specific programmes also increased.

About 16.9 per cent of the respondents who belonged to labour class did not try to get more information about their development schemes due to their lack of regular attendance in Gramasabha meetings. Most of them did not pay much attention to its function. The calculated χ^2 value for 6 degrees of freedom is 35.686, (corresponding p-value is 0.005). Hence we reject the null hypothesis and concluding that, there is a strong relationship between the occupation of the respondents and their knowledge about specific programs.

Monthly Income and knowledge of Specific Programs

Traditionally, substantial number of SC women has been denied access into educational institutions. Most of the time, they have been constrained to participate in the socio-cultural activities. Due to this social set up, SC women are unable to avail their basic education. Such a situation persuades them to seek their jobs in the urban areas. Such isolation and inequalities result in low income generation for the SC women. Inequalities in the occupation and variation in the income could play a major barrier in enhancing SC women's empowerment.

Table 3.7: Monthly income and knowledge of specific programmes

Monthly Income (Rs.)	Knowledge of Specific Programmes of SC Women				χ^2	df	p-value
	To Great Extent (%)	To some Extent (%)	Not at all (%)	Total			
501-1000	74 (46.8)	66 (41.8)	18 (11.4)	158	19.089**	4	0.005
1001-3000	53 (50.0)	41 (38.7)	12 (11.3)	106			
3001 above	31 (86.1)	5 (13.9)	–	36			
Total	158 (52.7)	112 (37.3)	30 (10)	300			

** Significant at 1% level (p<0.01)

The downtrodden SC women in the rural areas are not aware of the many programmes which were implemented, for their empowerment. The above table is related with the respondents monthly income and awareness about the programmes implemented for them. The table clearly shows that, the respondents studied who had a monthly income in the range of Rs. 3000 and above had better awareness. If their monthly income plunged below Rs. 3000, then we find their awareness level reduced by almost 50 per cent.

Last came the income group of Rs. 501-1000. Thus awareness level of the sample respondents descends on the basis of their monthly income. The calculated χ^2 value for 4 degrees of freedom is 19.089, (corresponding p-value = 0.005), Hence we reject the null hypothesis and concluding that, there is indeed a strong relationship between the respondent's monthly income and their knowledge about specific programs.

Support from other Agencies

The approach of the government to women's development was that of welfare and all the programmes for women were implemented through the Department of Social Welfare. The long term objective of the Integrated Women's Empowerment Programme (IWEP), was the all-round empowerment of women that is to uplift them socially and economically. Thus it could be gained their direct access and control over resources through a sustained process of mobilization and convergence of all in the ongoing sectoral programmes. The programmes are Balika Smridhi Yojana, Education Work for Prevention of Atrocities on Women, Anganwadi Workers Welfare Fund, Women's Welfare Services (WWS), Support Training and Employment Programme for Women (STEPW).There are different programmes for women in Kerala some under the Department of Social Welfare, some as part of the central government schemes, and still others from independent agencies. From the below table, it is quite evident that about 21.3 per cent of SC women get support from other agencies while a higher percentage of 78.7 do not receive any support from any agency. This fact was subjected to further analysis.

Education and Support from Agencies

Educating the women is the most powerful instrument of changing their position in the society. If you educate a woman, you are educating a family. Education brings about reduction in inequalities and also acts as a means of improving their status within the family. To bring more girl children, from the marginalized BPL families into the mainstream of education, Government has been providing package concessions in the form of free supply of books, uniform, boarding and lodging, clothing for hostelites, mid-day meals, scholarships and so on. The Kerala Government has initiated decentralized programmes for weaker sections among women to their social mobility. It is necessary that SC women come with domination and subordination for which they need to be educated and trained. The other agencies like NGOs serves as supporting structures for women and are very useful.

Table 3.8: Support from other agencies by education wise

Education	Support from other Agencies		Total	χ^2	df	p-value
	Yes (%)	No (%)				
Illiterate	16(28.6)	40(71.4)	56	35.494**	3	0.005
Primary	23(12.8)	156(87.2)	179			
Pre degree	11(25)	33(75)	44			
Graduate	14(66.7)	7(33.3)	21			
Total	64(21.3)	236(78.7)	300			

** Significant at 1% level ($p<0.01$)

From the analysis of SC women's awareness about the programmes which the government put forward to empower them is clear that, they were not aware as most of the respondents were illiterates. From the table above, it is noted that only the educated people get more support from other agencies. The support from the agencies declines according to their qualification. Only 28.6 per cent of illiterates said that they were supported by the agencies. 71.4 per cent of the illiterates were not supported and they did not know much about the agencies. But for a helping hand, these poor agencies never meet their needs. Among the sample respondents who were primarily educated about 87.2 per cent felt that they did not get any support from these agencies.

The agencies like NGO and Nehru Yuva Kendra are the agencies used as helping hands to empower the poor. It was not dynamic in its action. If these agencies function more actively, it would help the poor gain literacy. The calculated χ^2 value for 3 degrees of freedom was 35.494, for a corresponding p-value of 0.005. Hence, the null hypothesis is rejected and concludes that, there is a strong relationship between the respondent's age and the gain of support from various agencies.

Occupation and Support from other Agencies

It has been observed that women's status across the world has been changing over the time, with varying socio-economic impact of a family. As per World Bank Report, women must not be regarded as mere recipients of public support; they are first and foremost, economic agents (World Bank Report, 1992). It is also a worrisome reality that women are concentrated in more precarious forms of employment in which earning are low. Informal employment generally represents a large source of employment for women than men. In other words, women's participation can help to keep a family free of poverty.

Table 3.9: Occupation and support from other agencies

Occupation	Support from other Agencies			χ^2	df	p-value
	Yes (%)	No (%)	Total			
Employed	24 (44.4)	30 (55)	54	25.801**	3	0.005
Self employed	8 (17.4)	38 (82.6)	46			
Labour	26 (21)	98 (79)	124			
Unemployed	6 (7.9)	70 (92.1)	76			
Total	64 (21.3)	236 (78.7)	300			

** Significant at 1% level ($p<0.01$)

From the above table it becomes crystal clear that the employed respondents (44.4%) got more support from agencies. (Such as NYK, JSS, STED). The labour respondents (79%), self employed (82.6%) and almost all among the unemployed respondents (92.1%) were emphatic that they never got any support from any of these agencies. Only a minimum percentage of the respondents had any idea about the function and nature of these agencies. Hence awareness needs to be created regarding the same.

The calculated χ^2 value for 3 degrees of freedom regarding the same was found to be 25.801, at a corresponding p-value of 0.005. Hence, we reject the null hypothesis and conclude that, there exists a strong relationship between the respondent's occupation and the access to support from other related agencies.

Monthly Income and Support from Agencies

The government sponsored agencies have emerged as a vibrant support that has become part and parcel of the rural community. The rural India, at present is interlaced with the thickening web of such grassroots level organizations (Narayanaswamy, Manivel and Basker, 2005).

Table 3.10: Monthly income and support from other agencies

Monthly Income (Rs.)	Support from other Agencies		Total	χ^2	df	p-value
	Yes (%)	No (%)				
501-1000	12 4(48.5)	34 (21.5)	158	14.434**	2	0.005
1001-3000	96 (90.6)	10 (9.4)	106			
300 & above	36 (100)	–	36			
Total	85.3 (256)	44 (14.7)	300			

** Significant at 1% level ($p<0.01$)

It is also noteworthy that, though the government has taken many steps to create awareness, not many grassroot rural SC women are aware of many programmes. The above table depicts the awareness about the supporting agencies.

People in the income group of Rs. 3000 and above have shown positive results of about 100 percent about their awareness of such supporting programmes. This awareness level reduces to 90.6 per cent in the 1000-3000 income groups and dips further to (48.5%) in Rs. 501-1000 income group. Considering the government programme among rural SC women, this should have been reversed, and awareness should haven been increased among the lower income groups. Hence, one may question the awareness and insist on the supporting agencies doing something more to create awareness among the lower income groups in the future.

The calculated χ^2 value for 2 degrees of freedom was noted to be 14.434, at corresponding p-value of 0.005. Hence, the null hypothesis is rejected and concludes that, there is a strong relationship between the respondent's monthly income and the gain of support from other agencies.

Right to Speak in the Meeting

India is a country of much tradition and customs. Though the culture, traditions and customs have changed globally, Indian culture continues to be with little or no changes. One positive change that has come up is the status of women. Earlier women were meant to be confined to the kitchen, chauvinized by the male members. But off late she is respected, more noticed. She has begun to enjoy more of the rights as her male counterpart. From the table 3.11, it has been inferred that about 78.7 per cent of SC women did exercise the right to speak during meetings, while 21.3 per cent do not enjoy. This fact was further analysed with respect to the significant independent variables.

Family Type and Right to Speak

It has been observed that women's status across the globe has been changing over the time, with the varying socio-economic impact on the family. But the case of SC women is different; women still suppressed continue to be in the villages.

Table 3.11: Type of family and right to speak in the meeting

Family Type	Right to Speak		Total	χ^2	df	p-value
	Yes (%)	No (%)				
Joint family	131 (83.4)	26 (16.6)	157	4.471*	1	0.024
Nuclear family	105 (73.4)	38 (26.6)	143			
Total	236 (78.7)	64 (21.3)	300			

* Significant at 5% level ($p<0.05$)

From the above table, the respondents from the joint family (83.4%) claimed that they were bold enough to speak in the public meetings. They could communicate and articulate legibly, without making mistakes or bluffing. About 16.6 per cent of the joint family respondents and 26.6 per cent of the nuclear family respondents opined that they could not speak in the public meetings.

Thus, this problem of inhibition should be dealt with in our society. Women should be able to face anybody and anything in her life. This culture of silence and subordination must be eliminated from all society. The calculated value for χ^2 for 1 degree of freedom is 4.471, for the corresponding p-value of 0.024. Hence, the null hypothesis is rejected and concludes a strong relationship between the type of family and their right to speak in the public meetings.

Monthly Income and Right to Speak

Monthly income of women has been an important indicator of economic solvency as well as economic empowerment. In India women are mostly dependent on their husbands' income and their income is perceived to supplement the household income. Further more, women depend on their husband's decision for availing financial support. An attempt was made to examine the relationship between the income and the participation and articulation during meetings.

Table 3.12: Monthly income and willingness to speak during meetings

Monthly Income (Rs.)	Right to Speak		Total	χ^2	df	p-value
	Yes (%)	No (%)				
501-1000	23 (14.6)	135 (85.4)	158			
1001-3000	36 (34.0)	70 (66.0)	106	30.323**	2	0.005
3000 & above	20 (55.6)	16 (44.4)	36			
Total	79 (26.3)	221 (73.7)	300			

** Significant at 1% level ($p<0.01$)

The above table reveals that the respondents having a monthly income of Rs. 1000-3000 were volunteered to speak during public meetings. On the other hand, women from the lower income group were hesitant to voice their opinions. The women (55.6%) in the income group Rs. 3001 and above felt that they had more right to speak followed by 34 per cent of women in income group Rs. 1001-3000. But, only 14.6 per cent women belonging to the income group of Rs. 501-1000 income group spoke up. It is clear that the people who earn more monthly income were better able to articulate in the public.

The calculated value for χ^2 is for 2 degrees of freedom is 30.323, for a corresponding p-value is of 0.005. Hence, the null hypothesis is rejected and conclude that there is a strong relationship between the sample respondent's monthly income and their willingness to speak in the public meetings.

Greater Participation in Development Agencies resulted by Awareness

We further discussed the depth, quality and process of participation. The literature on participation has demonstrated that even in "mature" democracies, participation rates are highly uneven across socio-economic groups (Verba, Schlozman, and Brady, 1995) Educational development among SC women is very marginal because girls were often forbidden from going out as they had responsibilities at home. Therefore, gender discrimination starts at very early stages in the life of SC women. Normally, they are retained at home to look after the household chores. Generally in the male dominated society, lack of participation among SC women is quite natural. This confinement to the homes would predispose them to automatically unawareness. SHGs generally enhance the status of women as participants, decision-makers and beneficiaries in the democratic, economic, social and cultural spheres of life. It is found that SHGs inculcated a great confidence in the minds of rural women to succeed in their day to day life. (Ritu Jain, R.K. Kushawaha and A.K. Srivastava, 2003). Table 3.13 indicates that only a small percentage of SC women (21.3 %) were aware and so involved themselves and participated in programmes conducted by various development agencies. A relatively high percentage of about 78.7 percent because of the lack of awareness and did not participate in any programmes. Participation was further analysed with respect to a few significant independent variables.

Education and Participation

Educated women are actively participating in the activities of SHGs, NHGs, Gramasabha and other such agencies. Education enables them to enter into the public domain. Education can enrich the knowledge of the women and provides platform to enter into the public activities. The more recent days, find SHGs and NHGs members transforming into entrepreneurs. Many success stories revealed education has strong association in the public participation. Educated women have more opportunities to participate in the public forum.

Table 3.13: Education and greater participation in development agencies resulted by awareness

Education	Participation Resulted by Awareness		Total	χ^2	df	p-value
	Yes (%)	No (%)				
Illiterate	16 (28.6)	40 (71.4)	56	35.494**	3	0.005
Primary	23 (12.8)	156 (87.2)	179			
Pre degree	11 (25)	33 (75)	44			
Graduate	14 (66.7)	7 (33.3)	21			
Total	64 (21.3)	236 (78.7)	300			

** Significant at 1% level ($p<0.01$)

As far as the relation between education and participation in SHGs is concerned, the highest percentage (66.7%) of respondents hailed from the category of graduates. They showed more positive awareness, compared to category of the illiterates (28.6%) and matriculation (25%). respondents from the category of educated primary (87.2 %) demonstrated the least participation awareness.

The awareness is a key variable; it may vary from people to people according to their interaction with others. It is well recognized that the education is an important factor, having a decisive influence on one's awareness. From the present study the data relating to the educational attainment of the respondents who also happen to be the heads of households. By analyzing the relationship between educational attainment and awareness, educational attainment does not tend to be high. About 75 percent of respondents were not aware.

The calculated value for χ^2 is for 3 degree of freedom was found to be 35.494, for the corresponding p-value of 0.005. Hence, the null hypothesis is rejected and concludes that, there is a strong relationship between level of education and their participation vide the right to speak in the public meetings.

Family Type and Participation

In the rural development, it is necessary to take into account the factor of social participation. The social participation implies the ways in which members of the village community are able to express their solidarity, feelings in community life and community organizational participation through a multifarious activities including organizational participation in SHGs.

In India, traditionally women are considered to be home makers. She has to take care of all domestic affairs of her household. The joint family may provide enough time for women to participate in the public sphere. But in the nuclear family system, she may have little extra time to think about it. Today, joint family system has partially vanished from our society. Though women from the nuclear family had little time to participate in the public sphere, they enjoyed the freedom. Such freedom could lead to independence. It is further that tendency to empowerment.

Table 3.14: Type of family and greater participation in development agencies resulted by awareness

Family Type	Participation Resulted by Awareness		Total	χ^2	df	p-value
	Yes (%)	No (%)				
Joint family	128 (81.5)	29 (18.5)	157	18.780**	1	0.005
Nuclear family	139 (97.2)	4 (2.8)	143			
Total	267 (89)	33 (11)	300			

** Significant at 1% level ($p<0.01$)

The findings relating to the participation in local organisation are discussed in table 3.14. It reveals that 97.2 per cent of the respondents from the nuclear family took more interest and thus participated in the SHGs, a clear indicator of their awareness. On the other hand 81.5 percent of the sample respondents from the joint family showed interest in participation. This may be explained by the fact that the joint family being a large family; the female may be the income generators of the family. Her multiple roles in the family delimit her participation in the SHGs. Most of the SC women lived in joint families in the rural areas.

The presence and participation of SC women in SHGs brought about a formidable change in their position within the social organization, as well as in the overall hierarchal structure of the Indian society, leading towards their empowerment. In yester years, women were dependent on their husbands for support and assistance in every aspect of their life. Though women still face some restrictions, they are permitted to undertake jobs slowly.

The calculated value for χ^2 for 1 degree of freedom was found to be 18.780, and for the corresponding p-value is 0.005. Hence, the null hypothesis is rejected and conclude that, there is a strong relationship between the respondents type of family and participation in the developmental agencies resulted by awareness.

Occupation and Participation

Though women workers have made remarkable achievements in the country, considerable change among the women in SC community are not visible. Most of the menial jobs are carried out by these marginalized women. Yet they remain economically is very poor. In unorganized sector, SC women are categorized under daily wages. Few among more SC women engage in self employment schemes. This further leads to marginalization.

Table 3.15: Occupation and greater participation in development agencies resulted by awareness

Occupation	Participation Resulted by Awareness			χ^2	df	p-value
	Yes (%)	No (%)	Total			
Employed	34 (63.00)	20 (37)	54	49.408**	3	0.005
Self employed	41 (89.1)	5 (10.9)	46			
Labour	116 (93.5)	8 (6.5)	124			
Unemployed	76 (100.)	–	76			
Total	267 (89.0)	33 (11.)	300			

** Significant at 1% level ($p<0.01$)

The above table very clearly depicts the relation between the occupation and participation in SHGs. 100 percent of unemployed respondents were aware about SHGs and participated more in the programmes and opportunities they offered. However, in compassion only 93.5 percent of labourers participated in SHGs. The self employed respondents (89.1%) did slightly better than the unemployed respondents (63%). This clearly shows that better the awareness, as in the case of the unemployed here, higher the chance for their active participation.

The χ^2 value for is for 3 degrees of freedom was 49.408, for a corresponding p-value of 0.005. Hence, we reject the null hypothesis; conclude that, there is a strong relationship between the respondent's occupation and participation in the developmental agencies on account of their awareness.

Utilization and Awareness

The traditional skills of women have helped them to develop their income. These skills of women not only help to generate income but also generate awareness among other women. As they become members of SHGs/ NHGs, they engage in selling their products to other customers. This interaction exposed them to others and helped them to gain awareness about various support systems. Thus more women become aware and were likely to join such supportive systems. The below table shows that about 6 per cent of SC women have to great extent increased awareness about supportive systems through utilization, on the other hand, 69 per cent had to a certain extent spread awareness, while 25 per cent have no role to play in increasing awareness. This fact was further analysed with the significant independent variables as follows.

Age and Utilisation

Age plays a prominent role in marketing the products of SHGs/NHGs. People of a mature, middle age group experienced higher success when involved in marketing the products. Given the age and attained, the elder ones were able to market their products more successfully. Moreover, their persuasive spirit, determination, seriousness and involvement are very high compared to women from the younger age groups.

The people in the rural villages possessed many traditional skills and crafts. Not everybody had all the skills necessary; moreover their capabilities are not evenly distributed. The people who knew to design well, cook well, utilized all their ability in the SHGs to get good income. Their knowledge to do anything successfully in the SHGs are related to their age. The above table clearly reflects that the aged people with their experience in their life could put forth something better and more concrete, which will contribute to good income to the SHGs.

Table 3.16: Age and utilization increased awareness about supportive systems

Age	Utilization Increased Awareness				χ^2	df	p-value
	To Great Extent (%)	To Some Extent (%)	Not at all (%)	Total			
18-25	4 (8.2)	34 (69.4)	11 (22.4)	49			
26-33	5 (5.4)	72 (77.4)	16 (17.2)	93			
34-41	1 (1.2)	68 (82.9)	13 (15.9)	82	35.235**	6	0.005
42 Above	8 (10.5)	33 (43.4)	35 (46.1)	76			
Total	18 (6.0)	207 (69.0)	75 (25.0)	300			

** Significant at 1% level (p<0.01)

The respondents 42 and above (10.5%) felt that by utilizing the awareness and their capability in bringing new outcomes they could earn a lot. However the other age group categories ranging from 18-41 were less confident when compared to ones above 42 years.

The calculated value for χ^2 for 6 degrees of freedom was 35.235, for a corresponding p-value of 0.005. Hence, the null hypothesis is rejected and conclude that, there is a strong relationship between the respondent's age group, and the extent of utilization to support systems.

Family Type and Utilisation

Family members attitude heavily influence women's involvement in different government sponsored agencies. It is the male members who create opportunities for women to give forth and involve with development agencies.

Table 3.17: Type of family and utilisation increased by awareness, about supportive systems

Family Type	Utilization Increased Awareness				χ^2	df	p-value
	To Great Extent (%)	To Some Extent (%)	Not at All (%)	Total			
Joint family	15 (9.6)	98 (62.4)	44 (28)	157			
Nuclear family	3 (2.1)	109 (76.2)	31 (21.7)	143	10.207**	2	0.006
Total	18 (6)	207 (69)	75 (25)	300			

** Significant at 1% level (p<0.01)

The greater percent of the respondents (76.2%) hailed from the nuclear family. They recorded that their utilization awareness had increased to some extent. 9.6 per cent of the joint family members claim that the utilization level has increased to great extent, compared with the nuclear family (2.1 %) respondents, whose utilisation level is less.

The calculated value for χ^2 is for 2 degrees of freedom is 10.207, and the corresponding p-value is 0.006, and by rejected the null hypothesis and it can be conclude that, there is a strong relationship between the sample respondent's family type and by increasing their utilization awareness.

Monthly Income and Utilisation

The development of any community depends on the income they generate. It is proved that, income is the key to human progress and social change. It is a powerful tool for empowerment of an individual, and helps in instilling confidence in individual and community about their own capacities, inherent strength to shape their lives and thus enhance the inner strength, intellectual, political, social and economic against, oppression, exclusion and discrimination. In the context of the study, utilization implies the extent to which that people actively used their own production made by SHGs/NHGs. Thus, utilization is a process by which beneficiaries directly influence the implementation of development programmes in order to enhance prosperity in terms of income and personal growth, self-reliance or other values that they cherish.

Table 3.18: Monthly income and utilisation increased by awareness about supportive systems

Monthly Income	Utilization Increased Awareness				χ^2	df	p-value
	To Great Extent (%)	To Some Extent (%)	Not at all (%)	Total			
501-1000	11 (7)	107 (67.7)	40 (25.3)	158	10.849*	4	0.028
1001-3000	7 (6.6)	67 (63.2)	32 (30.2)	106			
3001 above	–	33 (91.7)	3 (8.3)	36			
Total	18 (6)	207 (69)	75 (25)	300			

* Significant at 5% level ($p<0.05$)

For the development of the SC women in the society the government took many measures, which despite all efforts remain underutilized. 7 per cent of the respondents in the category of Rs. 501-1000 have reported that their utilisation had been increased through awareness to a great extent. 67.7 per cent of the sample respondents have responded that their utilization had increased through awareness to some extent. While 25.3 per cent respondents have reported that they never utilized it at all.

The 6.6 per cent respondents is in the range of Rs. 1001-3000, had reported that they had utilized the supportive systems to great extent, 63.2 per cent of the respondents replied that they had utilised them to some extent, and finally the 30.2 per cent of the respondents said that they never utilised it. In the range of income Rs. 3001 and above, none of the respondents have reported that they utilized the supportive systems, 91.7 percent respondents had reported that to some extent they utilise them, and 8.3 percent of the respondents had informed that they never utilized them.

The calculated value for χ^2 at 4 degrees of freedom was found to be is 10.894, at the corresponding p-value of 0.028. Hence, the null hypothesis is rejected and it can be conclude that, there is a strong relationship between the sample respondents' monthly income and the increase in their utilization awareness.

Conclusion

Awareness generation is a capacity that enables an individual to seek information about any aspect of social reality through various sources. In this study awareness regarding various developmental programmes for the empowerment of SC women were sought from the respondents. About half of the respondents (53.3 %) had awareness to some extent about the functioning of government agencies and two fifth of the population (41.3%) had it to a great extent. The cross analysis with significant independent variable showed statistically significant associations. The cross table analysis also revealed that among the variables, the educated, the respondents from higher age at marriage, high income group had greater awareness than their counter parts.

About half of the respondents (52.7%) had awareness regarding the specific programmes of government to a great extent and 37.3 per cent had it to some extent. The cross analysis also showed highly significant statistical association with the variables like education, occupation and income. Among the categories of these variables higher level of awareness was found among the graduates, self employed and higher income categories.

Supports from other agencies are also very important in the process of empowering the marginalized sections of the community. But only 21.3 per cent got such support from the agencies outside the government and therefore it is an urgent concern for empowering the SC women. The cross table analysis showed statistically significant association with the variables such as education, occupation and income. Among the value points of these variables, the graduate, employed and high income groups tap more support from the outside agencies.

More than three fourth of the respondents (78.7%) were aware about their right to speak in the meetings or public forums. This is a positive indicator for empowering the SC variable determining this process. Among them the members from the joint family and high income categories showed more awareness.

Generally the participation in various programmes generate more awareness but in this study it did not have much significance as only less than one fourth of the respondents (21/3%) benefited in such a way. Education, family type and occupation had a significant role in the process. The more educated respondents and nuclear family members were more benefited from the participation.

The utilization of services increased the awareness to some extent for 69 per cent of the respondents. The cross table analysis showed that age, family type and monthly income had statistically significant association with the utilization of services. Among the variables, the middle aged groups, joint family members and high income group increased their level of awareness through the utilization of services than their respective counterparts.

The ANOVA results also showed that these independent variables are positively associated with the level of awareness. Among them, the education, family type and monthly income are highly correlated with the awareness level.

4

Social Empowerment of Scheduled Caste Women

Society's capacity for self-direction and control of community processes and resources are the key elements of social empowerment. It is an active multidimensional process, which should enable women to realize their full identity and power in all spheres of life. It would consist of greater access to knowledge and resources, greater autonomy in decision-making, greater ability to plan their lives, have greater control over the circumstances that influence their lives and free them from the shackles imposed on them by customs, beliefs and practices (Soni, 2001). Empowerment of the weaker sections such as SCs is an all-encompassing process that includes educational, economic, social, political and cultural spheres.

The Ministry of Welfare was constituted on 25th September, 1985 with an objective of empowering the socially and economically deprived sections of the society which was renamed as the Ministry of Social Justice and Empowerment on 25th May, 1998 (India, 2006). The Ministry of Social Justice and Empowerment undertakes multitudes of programmes in order to ensure social justice and empowerment of the disadvantaged sections such as the Scheduled Castes, Scheduled Tribes, Backward Classes and Minorities.

Social justice is an objective well established in the Preamble of the Indian Constitution, which demands preferential treatment to the weaker sections so as to set right the historical imbalances existing in the society. The Constitution of India directs the Governments, both the Central and State, to take positive actions to uplift the social, economic and educational status and to provide justice to the weaker sections so as to bring about equality. This has placed the need for empowerment of SCs at the center of thoughts in the socio-political circles in the country.

Through the concerted interventions of the Government and the Non-Governmental agencies or on account of their own autonomous efforts some changes have been brought about in the conditions of the weaker sections of Indian society. The mushrooming of women's organizations is a positive indicator. The LSGs' ultimate aim was to empower the people with the help of a change in the power structure and granting powers to the socially and politically powerless.

The National Commission for Scheduled Castes, a constitutional body monitors and safeguards the issues concerning their power and prestige. According to 2001 census, the population of the Scheduled Castes, one of the socially and economically most backward sections, was 16.16 crores, constituting 16.23 percent of the country's population. This social segment received social recognition with the Mandal Judgement in 1992. The Government of India and the State Governments have initiated numerous measures over the years to improve the conditions of this lot. However, they are miles away from the goals of education, health care and social identity even in the dawn of the 21st century.

Indian society is in a state of transition, experiencing tremendous changes in the social institutional structures. These changes have been well confirmed and rapid during the last few decades. The shift in the ideologies in international politics and market oriented economic policies of developed countries created a crisis in almost all the developing countries in the world, particularly in the last quarter of 20th century. These politics and policies insisted the developing countries to follow the model of the industrially advanced and developed nations. In line with this India too liberalized her policies and opened the market.

Empowerment is a multidimensional social process that helps people gain control over their own lives. It is a process that entrusts people with power (the capacity to implement) that can be used in their own lives, communities and society at large, by acting on issues that they consider as important. Above all, empowerment is the result of participation in the decision-making process (Saxena, N.C 2000). Women's empowerment, then, refers to the process by which women acquire due recognition on par with men, to participate in the development process of the society through the political institutions as a partner with human dignity (Palanithurai, G 2001).

Decision Making

Women's equality in power sharing and decision making, with special focus to political decision making process at all levels, needs to be ensured for the achievement of the goals of empowerment. Lack of social, political and economic empowerment deprives women from accessibility to resources, opportunities and decision making which in turn leads to greater impoverishment of the poor households (Mukherjee, N 1996). Necessary measures are to be taken so as to guarantee women equal access to and effective participation in decision making bodies in all areas, including the legislative, executive, judicial, corporate, statutory bodies, as also the advisory

Commissions, different Committees, Boards, and Trusts and so on. Affirmative actions such as reservations/quotas, especially in higher legislative bodies, need be considered whenever necessary on a time bound basis. Women friendly policies and processes should also be drawn up to encourage women to participate effectively in the developmental process.

Policies, programmes and systems, ensuring mainstreaming of women's perspectives in all developmental processes, as catalysts, participants and recipients have to be established. Wherever gaps in policies and programmes are experienced, women specific interventions would be undertaken. Coordination and monitoring mechanisms should also be devised from time to time to assess the progress of such mechanisms. Women issues and concerns, as a result, would specially be addressed and reflected in all concerned laws, sectoral policies, plans and programmes of action.

In the present study social empowerment of SC women are analysed and observations made on the basis of certain indicators. Among the social empowerment indicators, decision making capacity hold prime importance as it is the arena where one can utilize one's own resources at best. The respondents were asked about their level of decision making capacity before and after participation in the developmental programmes through PRIs. 54 per cent of the respondents rarely exercised their role in decision making, and a significant proportion of 33.7 per cent and 12.3 per cent exercised it often and very often respectively. This level of decision making, prior to the involvement in PRIs programmes, was low among the SC women in the area studied. This fact was further explored and analysed with the significant independent variables as follows.

Age and Decision Making

Age is an important demographic variable that decides the level of decision making within the family. The different age groups will have different experiences and that can play pivotal role in the decision making process. Although it is hard to get reliable information on party membership, it is widely recognized that women comprise only a small percentage of the membership in political parties. It is hardly surprising that women are invisible in the decision-making bodies and rarely influence significant policy decisions. Their under-representation in decision-making positions has serious implications for participation.

The table 4.1 shows that the decision making within the family has so often been done by the male members, which means that there is a constrained space available for women to take decision, particularly in age group of above 42 years. Only 26.3 per cent of the respondents in the age group above 42 years were able to make some decisions. But in the age group of 26-33 years, there was a significant increase in participation in decision making; about 44.1 per cent of this age group was able to participate in decision making.

Table 4.1: Age group and decision making before attending the government agencies

Age Group	Participation in Decision making Process in the Family				χ^2	df	p-value
	Very Often (%)	Often (%)	Rarely (%)	Total			
18-25	15 (30.6)	16 (32.7	18 (36.7)	49	28.290**	6	0.005
26-33	4 (4.3)	41 (44.1)	48 (51.6)	93			
34-41	7 (8.5)	24 (29.3)	51 (62.2)	82			
42 above	11 (14.5)	20 (26.3)	45 (59.2)	76			
Total	37 (12.3)	101 (33.7)	162 (54)	300			

** Significant at 1% level ($p<0.01$)

It is also seen that respondents of young age group i.e. 18-25 and of higher age group above 42 years had very less space in decision making. Only 16 percent in both the age groups were able to make decisions and implement it. This increased participation of the age groups ranging from 26-33 is the reflection of their education, occupation and economic advancement compared to the other categories. These factors have considerably increased their social space particularly in decision making within the family. This data also throws light on social awareness before attending Gramasabha, SHGs/NHGs.

The calculated Chi-square value for 6 degrees of freedom was estimated at 28.290; with the corresponding p-value of 0.005. It is clear that the relationship between the age of the SC women and their participation in the decision making process is highly significant. Hence we may reject the null hypothesis.

Education and Decision Making

Education entrusts SC women with the knowledge and moral power that enables them to take decisions within the family. This power can further be enhanced by providing them knowledge of government schemes and also by teaching them the methods of implementation. It is useful to remember that engendering state institutions does not invariably translate into gender equitable policies. This necessitates the creation of an enabling political, social and cultural environment in which women acquire the awareness, capabilities and education, to articulate their concerns, and an institutional environment that is receptive and responsive to such concerns. As such, participation is a more broad-based process which encompasses state-society interactions.

Table 4.2: Educational status and Decision making before attending the government agencies

Educational Status	Participation in Decision making Process in the Family				χ^2	df	p-value
	Often (%)	Very often (%)	Rarely (%)	Total			
Illiterate	18 (32.1)	10 (32.1)	28 (50)	56			
Primary	71 (39.7)	4 (2.2)	104 (58.1)	179			
Pre-degree	12 (27.3)	12 (27.3)	20 (45.5)	44	62.490**	6	0.005
Graduate	–	11 (52.4)	10 (47.6)	21			
Total	101 (33.7)	37 (12.3)	162 (54.)	300			

** Significant at 1% level ($p<0.01$)

The table clearly indicates that education can play a key role in the decision making process. Respondents with a minimum of primary education come around 37.9 per cent and they are able to make and implement decisions within the family. Only 27.3 per cent of respondents having education to the maximum of pre-degree level are able to make and implement decisions. Most of the respondents (179 out of 300) have education up to primary level. This is also an indication that they are constrained in the way of education. It is also noted that illiterate respondents have a marginal space in decision making.

Even though 56 out of the 300 respondents are illiterates, only 32.1 per cent are able to make decisions and successfully implement it. This is a clear indication that educational upliftment is a key factor in determining the role of women in decision making process inside the family. Attendance in the Grama Sabha SHGs/NHGs would considerably supplement their education and increase their space in social empowerment.The social empowerment of SC women cannot be realized without providing education. Education provides them accessibility to different empowerment programmes and makes them aware of the need for empowerment. The study gives a clear picture about the role of education in women's decision making power within the family.

The χ^2 value calculated for 6 degrees of freedom is 62.490 for a corresponding p-value of 0.005, making it necessary to reject the null hypothesis. Hence, it is clear that education of SC women and their socio-cultural empowerment are significantly related.

Age at Marriage and Decision Making

Marriage often restricts the freedom of decision making, mobility and economic independence. Marriage often limits their participation in SHGs/ NHGs. It cannot be ignored that educated spouses are found to encourage their partners' participation in the decision making and are willing to provide them more physical and economic space.

Table 4.3: Age at marriage and decision making before their attending in the government agencies

Age at Marriage	Participation in Decision making Process in the Family				χ^2	df	p-value
	Very Often (%)	Often (%)	Rarely (%)	Total			
Blow 18 years	7 (14.9)	13 (27.7)	27 (57.4)	47	21.684**	4	0.005
18-21	4 (3.1)	50 (38.5)	76 (58.5)	130			
22 above	25 (22.5)	32 (28.8)	54 (48.6)	111			
Total	36 (12.5)	95 (33)	157 (54.4)	288			

** Significant at 1% level ($p<0.01$)

The table clearly shows that marriage at higher age certainly increases women's participation in decision making. The age group ranging from 18 to 21 years seems to have more opportunities to take decisions. Marriage at lower ages i.e., below 18 years, shows the tendency of their dependence on other family members in taking decisions. Whereas 27.7 per cent of them had the freedom to often make decisions, only 14.9 per cent of them very often make decisions. Late marriage also indicates increased independency of women. Among the respondents in the age group above 22 years, 51.3 per cent did partake in decision making and its implementation at household level. This show those ages of marriage is certainly an enabling variable that helps SC women in their participation in decision making and its implementation. The Gramasabha, SHGs/NHGs, by providing opportunities for effective participation in decision making processes, provide a platform to practice their role in socio-cultural realms. Generally the prevailing socio-cultural circumstances forbid women to take bold decisions within the context of the family. They prefer to be better partners who never oppose or speak against their husbands or family members' decision.

The χ^2 value calculated at 4 degrees of freedom is 21.684 with a corresponding p-value of 0.005. Hence we reject the null hypothesis, it is clear that the age at marriage of the SC women and their social empowerment is significantly related.

Family Type and Decision Making

The Indian family systems are complex and hierarchical. Women and younger members of the family usually play little role in decision making and discussions. They have to obey the decisions of the head of the family, who is normally a male member. The male members of the family are considered the bread winners and hence expected to have the final say. The scenario is gradually getting changed with the female members supporting the family and sometimes earning more income than the male members. Earning members have a valuable say in the family affairs which is being generally accepted by the entire family. The nuclear families with less hierarchy gives more physical and economic freedom, and of course freedom in decision making.

Table 4.4: Family Type and decision making before attending the government agencies

Family Type	Participation in Decision making Process in the Family				χ^2	df	p-value
	Very often (%)	Often (%)	Rarely (%)	Total			
Joint family	27 (17.2)	44 (28)	86 (54.8)	157	9.469**	2	0.009
Nuclear family	10 (7)	57 (39.9)	76 (53.1)	143			
Total	37 (12.3)	101 (33.7)	162 (54)	300			

** Significant at 1% level ($p<0.01$)

It is observed that about 39.9 per cent of the respondents belonging to nuclear families were able to make decisions and implement it. This is due to the relative absence of a hierarchical structure, prevalence of shared responsibility, and freedom of space in decision making in the nuclear family. On the contrary, in joint families there is more hierarchy and less physical, economic and social space in the decision making of the respondents. Only 28 per cent of the joint family members are able to make decisions and implement it.

The χ^2 value calculated for 2 degrees of freedom is 9.469 with the corresponding p-value of 0.009. Hence we reject the null hypothesis. It is clear that the family type of the SC women and their social empowerment is significantly related.

Occupation and Decision Making

Employment will certainly boost the confidence level of women. The employed SC women who support their families find it easier to take and implement their own decisions. But this never happens in the case of SC women particularly for those who are employed as labourers.

In the study, most of the respondents being labourers (124 out of 300 respondents) but only 36.3 per cent of them enjoyed share in decision making. Whereas in the case of the self-employed and the employed, though less in number, 50 per cent enjoy their share in decision making. About 34.8 per cent of the self-employed, and 31.5 per cent of the employed have share in decision making. This is high when compared to the total number of respondents in this category. This is a clear indication that employment gained through education is more respected within the family and their decisions are accepted and implemented more easily. Employment will give more space in the socio-cultural empowerment. Employment can be generated through Gramasabha, SHGs/NHG which would give decision making power to SC women.

Table 4.5: Employment status and decision making before attending the government agencies

Employment Status	Participation in Decision making Process in the Family				χ^2	df	p-value
	Very often (%)	Often (%)	Rarely (%)	Total			
Employed	21 (38.9)	17 (31.5)	16 (29.6)	54	50.545**	6	0.005
Self employed	1 (2.2)	16 (34.8)	29 (63)	46			
Labour	13 (10.5)	45 (36.3)	66 (53.2)	124			
Unemployed	2 (2.6)	23 (30.3)	51 (67.1)	76			
Total	37 (12.3)	101 (33.7)	162 (54)	300			

** Significant at 1% level (p<0.01)

The χ^2 value calculated for 6 degrees of freedom is 50.545 for a corresponding p-value of 0.005.Hence we reject the null hypothesis making it persistable to conclude that the employment status of the SC women and the extent of social empowerment are significantly related.

Monthly Income and Decision Making

The income generated from employment seems to improve the socio-economic status of SC women. The money has sometimes earned them acceptance and respect in the family. The money gives them confidence and self-respect, which is reflected in their role in decision making within the family.

Table 4.6: Monthly income and decision making before attending the government programmes

Monthly Income (Rs.)	Participation in Decision making Process in the Family				χ^2	df	p-value
	Very often (%)	Often (%)	Rarely (%)	Total			
501-1000	10 (6.3)	59 (37.3)	89 (56.3)	158	71.054**	4	0.005
1001-3000	7 (6.6)	37 (34.9)	62 (58.5)	106			
3001 above	20 (55.6)	5 (13.9)	11 (30.6)	36			
Total	37 (12.3)	101 (33.7)	162 (54)	300			

** Significant at 1% level (p<0.01)

The respondents in the income group of Rupees 1001-3000 have less percentage share in decision making. Most of them draw monthly earnings by doing odd jobs. Only 6.6 per cent were able to exercise their role in decision making. Majority of respondents came under the salary group of 501-1000. About 158 of the total respondents fall under this category. Most of them are labourers, who enjoy less social space. Hence, their participation in decision making is also less. Only 6.3 per cent were able to contribute in decision-making. Only 36 respondents of the total respondents fall under the higher income group. Most of them were either employed or self-employed and about 55.6 per cent often took decisions themselves.

The χ^2 value calculated at 4 degrees of freedom was 71.054, and for a corresponding p-value of 0.005, making it imperative to reject the null hypothesis. Hence, it is clear that the monthly income of the SC women and their socio-cultural empowerment are significantly related.

Decision Making after Attending the Government Programmes

PRIs are concerned as the effective platform for pooling up the local resources as well as mobilizing the untapped resources for the overall welfare of the community with special emphasis on the marginalized or weaker segments in the society. The SC women constitute the weakest among all the marginalized groups and special care needs to be taken to empower them from the planning agencies as well as the grass root governing mechanisms. 46.3 per cent of the respondents opined that their decision making capacity increased to some extent and for 44.3 percent of them it remained constant. Participation in various governmental initiatives have boosted the decision making capacities of a significant proportion of the SC women and thus the empowerment process is certainly influenced by these activities. This fact was further cross tabulated with significant independent variables.

Age Category and Decision Making after Attending Programmes

Participation in government sponsored programmes influences the socio-economic status and personal freedom of SC women. Exposure to government programmes can provides them with confidence in decision-making. It ascertains their individual freedom and the public participation. It is also evident that age factor is also an important variable in the decision making process.

Table 4.7: Age category and decision making after attending the government programmes

Age	Participation in Decision making Process in the Family						χ^2	df	p-value
	Increased to Great Extent (%)	Increased to Some Extent (%)	Remained the Same (%)	Decreased to Some Extent (%)	Decreased to Great Extent (%)	Total			
18-25	–	28 (57.1)	20 (40.8)	–	1 (2)	49	23.511**	12	0.024
26-33	5 (5.4)	38 (40.9)	42 (45.2)	6 (6.5)	2 (2.2)	93			
34-41	6 (7.3)	33 (40.2)	43 (52.4)	–	–	82			
Above 42	7 (9.2)	40 (52.6)	28 (36.8)	1 (1.3)	–	76			
Total	18 (6)	139 (46.3)	133 (44.3)	7 (2.3)	3 (1)	300			

** Significant at 5% level ($p<0.05$)

The SHGs and NHGs have provided a unique opportunity for SC women in their upliftment. The SHG/NHG programmes have given them space to interact and provides knowledge about the government programmes executed for their upliftment. After attending SHGs/NHGs there is a considerable increase among the higher age category in decision making. About 52.6 percent of this age group was able to take decisions after attending Gramasabha, SHGs/NHGs. The opportunities offered by these group activities are mainly utilized by the higher age groups which manifests in their increased physical, economic and social freedom. Their decisions are being accepted and implemented inside their families. Even though there is an increase in the lower age group attending in Gramasabhas, SHGs/NHGs, their decision making level is lower compared to the higher age group. This may be because their mobility still requires the consent of other members in the family. Participation in Gramasabha, SHGs/NHG has enables their empowerment and its impacts will be extended to other areas.

The χ^2 value calculated for 12 degrees of freedom is 23.511 with a corresponding p-value of 0.024 rejecting the null hypothesis. It is clear that the age of the SC women and their participation in the decision making in the family is highly significant.

Education and Decision Making after Attending the Programmes

Education is the powerful tool to transform the socio-economic status of SC women. Participation in the government programmes can give hope and freedom to SC women. The enriched SC women can take firm decision within and outside their families. Involvement in SHGs/NHGs/Gramasabha acts as the enabling factor in this regard.

A higher educational attainment of citizens is an important prerequisite for performing greater role in political process (Meheta Ashok, 1979). Education enables one to act rationally. Previous studies in the area proved that higher education leads to greater commitment. In the opinion of Jorgan, education is not to be regarded as an important factor for participation in government programmes. Duverger is convinced that education is the most decisive factor for women's political participation. For the purpose of the present study, women in the sample are divided into four categories.

Participation in Gramasabha, SHGs/NHGs has increased the thirst of women for knowledge. Education has opened up a space to interact, communicate and to make wise decisions. Education also helped them to go through literatures and documentation available on empowerment. This has a positive impact, both qualitative and quantitative, on their decision making skill. As most of the respondents have only primary education, their decision making capacity has increased significantly after attending Gramasabha, SHGs/NHGs. About 43.6 per cent of the respondents having primary education were able to contribute in decision making in their family. With higher education this percentage tends to go up. About all of the respondents have reported that their involvement in the decision making process has increased after attending Gramasabha, SHGs/NHGs.

Table 4.8: Education and decision making after attending the government programmes

Education	Participation in Decision making Process in the Family					
	Increased to a Great Extent (%)	Increased to Some Extent (%)	Remained the Same (%)	Decreased to Some Extent (%)	Decreased to a Great Extent (%)	Total
Illiterate	3 (5.4)	21 (37.5)	31 (55.4)	1 (1.8)	–	56
Primary	11(6.1)	78 (43.6)	85 (47.5)	3 (1.7)	2 (1.1)	179
Pre-degree	4 (9.1)	19 (43.2)	17 (38.6)	3 (6.8)	1 (2.3)	44
Graduate	–	21 (100)	–	–	–	21
Total	18 (6)	139 (46.3)	133(44.3)	7 (2.3)	3 (1)	300

** Significant at 1% level ($p<0.01$) c^2 =34.153, df = 12, p-value = 0.001

The Gramasabha SHGs/NHGs have also improved the performance of illiterate in the process. About 37.5 per cent of the illiterate were able to make decisions of their own to some extent. The decision made by them is mainly on household matters like food, number of children, education of children etc. The participation has also given them confidence in joint decisions making along with other family members. The attendance has definitely increased the spouse relations and several relations in a positive way.

The χ^2 value for 12 degrees of freedom is 34.153, for the corresponding p-value of 0.001. Hence we reject the null hypothesis. It becomes clear that the education of the SC women and their socio-cultural empowerment are significantly related.

Age at Marriage and Decision making after Attending Programmes

In India, children are usually married at an early age; although the consummation of marriages will take place at a later age. Age at marriage is an important determinant in the decision making process in the case of women. It is also essential for women empowerment.

In the Indian cultural context early marriage can catapult woman from being a child to a woman with household and reproduction obligations. Early marriage disempowers women by curtailing their opportunity for higher education and skills formation. So, normally early marriage reduces their ability to make decisions both within the family and outside. The respondents' attendance in the Gramasabhas, SHGs/NHGs increased their capability in decision making. About 41.4 per cent of the respondents who married after 22 years of age had said that their decision making capacity have remained the same even after attending the SHGs /NHGs. The respondents, who married at the lower age, between of 18-21years, had shown improvements. The Gramasabhas, SHGs/NHGs have provided them with opportunities, physical space, economic space and social space. This enabled them to interact in the groups and come with wise decisions that expected to benefit the whole group and family. This has certainly boosted their self-confidence and helped them to make suggestions and implement the decisions.

Table 4.9: Age at marriage and decision making after attending the government programmes

Age at Marriage	Participation in Decision making Process in the Family					
	Increased to a Great Extent (%)	Increased to Some Extent (%)	Remained the Same (%)	Decreased to Some Extent (%)	Decreased to Great Extent (%)	Total
Below 18 years	3 (6.4)	28 (59.6)	14(29.8)	–	2 (4.3)	47
18-21	13 (10)	60 (46.2)	54 (41.5)	3 (2.3)	–	130
22 above	2 (1.8)	46 (41.4)	59 (53.2)	4 (3.6)	–	111
Total	18 (6.3)	134 (46.5)	127 (44.1)	7 (2.4)	2 (7)	288

** Significant at 1% level ($p<0.01$) $\chi^2 = 25.255$, df = 8, p-value = 0.001

The χ^2 value at 8 degrees of freedom is found to be 25.255 with the corresponding p-value of 0.001, making it imperative to reject the null hypothesis. It is therefore clear that the age at marriage of the SC women and their empowerment by way of participation in decision making in the family are significantly related.

Family Type and Decision Making after Attending Programmes

All the major aspects of women's life and the role they perform are determined within the boundaries of the family and married life. Traditionally, an Indian married woman's world is her home. She is required primarily to look after the welfare of her husband, progeny and other members of the family. The husband is expected to assume full responsibility for making arrangement for the provision and protection of the family. Thus, the husband–wife relationship in a traditional Indian family has been "male-dominance; female-dependence" (Kapur, 1970). Women have only marginal say in the policy matters or the decision making process of the family.

Nuclear families are households in which women reside alone or with her spouse with or without children. All other types of households are defined to be non-nuclear. Nuclear families are mostly families with women in the age group of 25-39. The nuclear families have large physical space for them to involve in the decision making and its implementation processes. Women's involvement in the said processes has a diametrically opposite relationship with the level of their dependency on other family members especially men. After attending Gramasabha/SHGs/NHG about 40 per cent of respondents from the nuclear family said that their ability to make decision has increased either to a great extent or to some extent. In spite of many drawbacks, the participation of nuclear family members in Gramasabha /SHGs/NHG will certainly increase their physical, economic and social freedom.

Table 4.10: Family type and decision making after attending the government programmes

Family Type	Participation in Decision making Process in the Family					
	Increased to a Great Extent (%)	Increased to Some Extent (%)	Remained the Same (%)	Decreased to Some Extent (%)	Decreased to Great Extent (%)	Total
Joint family	5 (3.2)	82 (52.2)	67 (42.7)	–	3 (1.9)	157
Nuclear	13 (9.1)	57 (39.9)	66 (46.2)	7 (4.9)	-	143
Total	18 (6)	139 (46.3)	133 (44.3)	7 (2.3)	3 (1)	300

** Significant at 1% level ($p<0.01$) $\chi^2 = 17.444$, df = 4, p-value = 0.002

The χ^2 calculated for 4 degrees of freedom is 17.444 for the corresponding p-value of 0.002. Hence we reject the null hypothesis. It is clear that the relation between family type of the SC women and their involvement in decision making after attending government programmes are highly significant.

Occupation and Decision Making after Attending Programmes

The economic status of the women respondents has influenced their share in decision-making. The economic status which has a linear relationship with occupation is an important factor to be analysed. As most of the respondents are either illiterates or have education at primary level or below, they could get employed only as labourers. Respondents with higher education seek employment in firms and establishments which could provide them regular a monthly income, others were self-employed. The unemployed category, which comes to 76 out of the 300 respondents, said that their participation in decision making had increased.

About 56.6 per cent of the unemployed category expressed that participation in government programmes helped them to improve their capacity to participate in the decision making process to some extent. This is because the unemployed, when given an opportunity to interact, make suggestions, make decisions and implement the decisions. Level of participation in the employed category was also increased to some extent. About 70.4 per cent of the employed respondents said that their role in decision making and implementation has increased to some extent. This trend is also true in the case of self-employed group. About 34.8 per cent of the self-employed respondents said that they had positive role in the decision making and in its implementation. So, employment had given them some financial base, confidence, and self-esteem, which has certainly increased their role in decision making.

Table 4.11: Occupation and decision making after attending the government programmes

Occupation	Participation in Decision making Process in the Family					
	Increased to a Great Extent (%)	Increased to Some Extent (%)	Remained the Same (%)	Decreased to Some Extent (%)	Decreased to Great Extent (%)	Total
Employed	1 (1.9)	38 (70.4)	12 (22.2)	3 (5.6)	–	54
Self employed	7 (15.2)	16 (34.8)	19 (41.3)	4 (8.7)	–	46
Labour	10 (8.1)	42 (33.9)	69 (55.6)	–	3 (2.4)	124
Unemployed	–	43 (56.6)	33 (43.4)	–	–	76
Total	18 (6)	139 (46.3)	133 (44.3)	7 (2.3)	3 (1)	300

** Significant at 1% level ($p<0.01$) $\chi^2 = 56.391$, df = 12, p-value = 0.000

The χ^2 value calculated at 12 degrees of freedom is 56.391 for the corresponding p-value of 0.000.Hence we reject the null hypothesis. It is clear that the occupation of the SC women and their social empowerment by way of participation in decision making after attending government programmes are highly significant.

Monthly Income and Decision Making after Attending Programmes

Gramasabhas/SHGs/NHGs have given some employment opportunity for the unemployed women. This source of employment has a corresponding impact on the level of participation of SC women. The extent of acceptance of their decisions by other members of the family and society at large is yet to be studied.

Table 4.12: Monthly income and decision making after attending the government programmes

Monthly Income (Rs.)	Participation in Decision making Process in the Family					
	Increased to a Great Extent (%)	Increased to Some Extent (%)	Remained the Same (%)	Decreased to Some Extent (%)	Decreased to a Great Extent (%)	Total
501-1000	7 (4.4)	53 (33.5)	93 (58.9)	3 (1.9)	2 (1.3)	158
1001-3000	9 (8.5)	58 (54.7)	34 (32.1)	4 (3.8)	1 (0.9)	106
3001 above	2 (5.6)	28 (77.8)	6 (16.7)	–	–	36
Total	18 (6)	139 (46.3)	133 (44.3)	7 (2.3)	3 (1)	300

** Significant at 1% level ($p<0.01$) $\chi^2 = 36.339$, df = 8, p-value = 0.000

The attendance in Gramasabha/SHGs/NHGs had not only provided income, but also a physical space to interact. The respondents with higher salary scale i.e.; 3001 and above had shown greater participation within the family and have their decisions implemented. About 77.8 per cent of this higher income group said that their role in decision making process has increased to some extent after attending the Gramasabha/SHGs/NHGs. The respondents with lower income have also shown greater participation. About 33.5 per cent of this group confirmed their role in participation, particularly in the family affairs, day to day domestic affairs, sexual relations and family planning. It is to be specially noted that the percentage of respondents who could improve their level of participation in the decision making in this income category is meagre. Less than 10 per cent in all income groups said that their level of participation has increased to a great extent. This may be due to the general constraints that prevail in their social space. Most women tended to deny that they have the master role in decision making, thus trying to express their respect towards their partners and elder members in the family; an expression of the social desirability component.

Only a small improvement has been reported after attending the programs. Hence it can be inferred that mere participation in SHGs/NHGs does not give enough moral confidence to SC women in decision making within the family.

The χ^2 value calculated at 8 degrees of freedom is 36.339 for the corresponding p-value of 0.000. Hence we reject the null hypothesis. It is clear that the monthly income of the SC women and their participation in decision making as an indicator of social empowerment are significantly related.

Naila Kabeer says that empowerment is a process, which entails change at different levels and different dimensions, it can be acquired at individuals in the inner self, it can acquire in relationship within family and household. It reflects in the capacity of women to determine agenda and make decisions in the family. Kabeer. N's emphasis in the collective grassroots level participation is the power to control others and resources. Women have the capacity to bargain, negotiate, and resist changes. The SHGs provide resources for these poor women, which in turn lead to strong agencies (decision making) and finally more achievements in their life.

Preference for Male Child

Preference for the male child is a significant negative social indicator that has a greater bearing on the empowerment of women. In a patriarchal society like Kerala, there is an inclination towards male children. When women themselves think of girl child as a burden, the empowerment of this segment itself is jeopardized. In the present study such an enquiry was made among the SC women and interestingly 78 percent of the respondents opined negatively that they did not prefer male child as their offspring. Only 13 per cent and 9 per cent of the respondents preferred male child over female to some extent and to a great extent respectively. This trend could be equated to the level of social empowerment. This factor was further cross tabulated with significant variables such as education and income.

Education and Preference for Male Child

Gender disparity manifests itself in various forms, the most obvious being the trend of continuously declining female ratio in the population in the last few decades. Social stereotyping and violence at the domestic and societal levels are some of the other manifestations. Discrimination against girl children, adolescent girls and women persists in many parts of the country. Empowerment can be only achieved through education and awareness. Education plays an important role in the empowerment process, especially that of women. In this study researcher had attempted to study the influence of education campaigning on the preference for a male child by SC women and the result is presented in the table 4.13.

Table 4.13: Education and preference for male child

Education	Preference for Male Child				χ^2	df	p-value
	To a Great Extent (%)	To Some Extent (%)	Not at all (%)	Total			
Illiterate	2 (3.6)	18 (32.1)	36 (64.3)	56	28.520**	6	0.005
Primary	22 (12.3)	17 (9.5)	140 (78.2)	179			
Pre-degree	3 (6.8)	3 (6.8)	38 (86.4)	44			
Graduate	–	1 (4.8)	20 (95.2)	21			
Total	27 (9.0)	39 (13.0)	234 (78.0)	300			

** Significant at 1% level ($p<0.01$)

Gender discrimination starts at the very early stage in the life of a Dalit girl. Normally girl children are retained at home to look after her younger siblings. The male in the family is usually the bread winner. The female has little physical space because of this and the position of women is continuously deteriorating. Joint family system, polygamy, property structure and early marriage are the hurdles in the development of women, particularly in Dalit community. So the family prefers the male child over female ones because the male members could supplement the family. In the process of decentralization there was a clear focus on gender. The amended of constitution mandates one third representation for women particularly in political institutions like village Panchayat or Grama Panchayat; giving adequate representation to women who helped people to accept a child and provide them equal opportunity and status in the family. The role played by the conventional education in giving the girl child equal status with that of male child is great. The educational propaganda taken by Gramasabha/SHGs/NHG has also educated the illiterate in gender equality. About 64.3 per cent of the illiterate respondents said that they had no special preference for male children. About 32 per cent of them had some preference for male child. About 78.2 per cent of the primary educated said that they had no special preference for male child. Most of the respondents had only primary education. The table clearly shows that respondents with higher education showed no preference for a male child. The education particularly by Gramasabha/SHGs/NHG, have definitely increased their sense of gender equality. The family is now able to recognise and accept the girl child. It is also understood that with opportunity for education, the girl child can also be a family bread winner.

The χ^2 calculated at 6 degrees of freedom is 28.520 for a corresponding p-value of 0.005.Hence we reject the null hypothesis. Hence, it is clear that the education of SC women and their preference for male child are significantly related.

Monthly Income and Preference for Male Child

Family income plays a major role in the decision making process. It is also a deciding factor in the life style of SC women and their empowerment structure. With this in the backdrop, the researcher attempted to investigate the preference for male child with the income of the respondents and the result is presented in table 4.14.

Table 4.14: Monthly income and preference for male child

Monthly Income (Rs.)	Preference for Male Child				χ^2	df	p-value
	To a Great Extent (%)	To Some Extent (%)	Not at all (%)	Total			
501-1000	22 (13.9)	23 (14.6)	113 (71.5)	158	13.815**	4	0.008
1001-3000	5 (4.7)	14 (13.2)	87 (82.1)	106			
30001 above	–	2 (5.6)	34 (94.4)	36			
Total	27 (9)	39 (13)	234 (78)	300			

** Significant at 1% level ($p<0.01$)

The above table clearly shows that neither the low income group nor higher income group shows preference for male child. Only but about 22 per cent of the low income group showed great preference for male child. Education and knowledge provide the awareness about gender equality, and SHGs and NHGs in current form play their due role in this sensitization process.

The χ^2 value calculated for 4 degrees of freedom is 13.815 at corresponding p-value of 0.008. Hence we reject the null hypothesis. Thus, it is clear that the variables vide, monthly income of the SC women and their preference for male child are related significantly.

Travelling without Male Escorts

In the traditional Kerala cultural context, women were often accompanied with the male members basically for their protection, but that in itself limits their freedom of movement. Traditional norms also devalue women and exclude them from decision-making and place them in a secondary position (Seth, 2001). In the process of empowerment, travelling alone to the outer social world is a common characteristic of women lot. This is evident in the findings; 85.3 per cent of the respondents agree with the statement while around 14.7 per cent disagree, which shows that empowerment of SC women manifests an increasing trend. This is further analysed with the significant independent variables.

Age and the need to be Accompanied by Male Escorts

Age determines the need for escorts for every human being in social as well as other activities. Different age groups require different levels of escort. Here the researcher has attempted to analyse the correlation between age and need for escorts through a field study and is presented in table 4.15.

Table 4.15: Age and travel without male escorts before participation in developmental agencies

Age	Travel without Male Escorts			χ^2	df	p-value
	Yes (%)	No (%)	Total			
18-25	47 (95.9)	2 (4.1)	49	8.000*	3	0.046
26-33	73 (78.5)	20 (21.5)	93			
34-41	70 (85.4)	12 (14.6)	82			
42 Above	66 (86.8)	10 (13.2)	76			
Total	256 (85.3)	44 (14.7)	300			

* Significant at 5% level ($p<0.05$)

Gramasabha/SHGs/NHGs are co-coordinated inside the village, so most respondents are able to reach Gramasabha/SHGs/NHGs without any help in terms of escorts or vehicles. Most often the location is at walkable distance, which allows the respondents to reach the Gramasabha/SHG/NHG without using a vehicle for transportation. Attending Gramasabha has made them confident enough to travel alone to some extent. 95.9 per cent in the 18-25 years age group and 86.8 per cent in the above 42 years age group travelled alone to Gramasabha without any male escorts. Most of the respondents enjoyed freedom to travel alone particularly to attend SHGs/

NHGs/Gramasabha. This freedom was granted to the respondents because their places of meeting were in close proximity to their residence. The people who participated in the Gramasabha/SHGs/NHGs know each other and often belong to the same society. Moreover, the meetings lasted for few hours and they could return home before it is too late. The table clearly shows that above 75 per cent of the respondents from the different age groups were allowed to travel to short distance and to Gramasabha/SHGs/ NHG without any escorts.

The χ^2 value calculated for 3 degrees of freedom is 8.000 for which the corresponding p-value of 0.046. Hence we may reject the null hypothesis. From this it is clear that the age of the SC women and their need to be accompanied by male escorts are significantly related variables.

Education and the need to be Accompanied by Male Escorts

Education plays a major role among the respondents as well as public in awareness building. Empowerment of women can be achieved only through proper education. With this backdrop, the researcher has attempted to find out the travel without escort before their participation in the developmental agencies and is presented in the table 4.16.

Table 4.16: Education and travel without male escorts before participating in the developmental agencies

Education	Travel without Male Escorts			χ^2	df	p-value
	Yes (%)	No (%)	Total			
Illiterate	45 (80.4)	11 (19.6)	56	9.000*	3	0.025
Primary	148 (82.7)	31 (17.3)	179			
Pre-degree	42 (95.5)	2 (4.5)	44			
Graduate	21 (100)	–	21			
Total	256 (85.3)	44 (14.7)	300			

* Significant at 5% level ($p<0.05$)

The table clearly shows that the respondents with higher education enjoyed complete freedom to travel alone, particularly to short distances; usually from house to place of work and back to home. They have begun to enjoy a limited freedom in travelling to distant places from where they can return within a day. Most of the illiterate were only allowed to travel from their place of work to their residence and to do some local shopping. Most of the respondents were confident enough to travel alone at least from their place of work to their residence. Their confidence to traveling alone has significantly increased by attending the NHGs and the SHGs.

The χ^2 value calculated for 3 degrees of freedom is 9.000 for a corresponding p-value of 0.025. Hence we reject the null hypothesis. From this it is clear that the education of the SC women and their need to be accompanied by male escorts significantly related.

Family Type and the need to be Accompanied by Male Escorts

Family type often determines the perception of security of its individual members. Women feel secured in the joint families whereas nuclear family poses some extent of risk in their security. This theory has been analysed among the respondents and the result is presented in table 4.17.

Table 4.17: Family type and travel without male escorts before participating in the developmental agencies

Family type	Travel without Male Escorts			χ^2	df	p-value
	Yes (%)	No (%)	Total			
Joint family	125 (79.6)	32 (20.4)	157			
Nuclear family	131 (91.6)	12 (8.4)	143	0.002**	1	0.002
Total	256 (85.3)	44 (14.7)	300			

* Significant at 1% level (p<0.01)

Respondents from the joint family face constraints in their travel. They need permission not only from their spouses but also from elder members of the family. Objection from any one of them may not allow them to travel alone. Only 79.6 per cent from the joint family were allowed to travel alone. But about 91.6 per cent of the respondents from nuclear family said that they travelled without any male escorts. This is because most of the respondents from the nuclear family need permission from only their spouses. The other family members do not have a say on them. The nuclear family assigns more responsibility on women, which demands them to travel without any male escorts.

The χ^2 value calculated for 1 degree of freedom is 0.002 for the corresponding p-value of 0.002. Hence we reject the null hypothesis, making it clear that the family type from which the SC women hail and their need to be accompanied by male escorts are significantly related.

Participation in Social Service Activities

Women participation in social service activities is directly related to their social empowerment. Higher the participation higher will be the empowerment of the subjects. The PRIs and the developmental initiatives open up in many forums for social engagements.

Most of the respondents in the study have less exposure to social work groups. Their social work activity is limited to local clubs and organizations. Despite their educational and other advancements, SC women still face major obstacles in holding a higher position in the society. Even though women's political participation has been made sure by the constitution, SC women are poorly represented in the social work groups as there are limited effective social service agencies in their locality. Their activity is limited to clubs like Nehru Yuva Kendra, and local sports and arts clubs. They are poorly represented even in these organizations.

Education and Social Service Activities

It is important to recognize that basic education is necessary for empowerment. There is no automatic mechanism to ensure it. Education is the only gateway to promote critical thinking among women. Entry of women in the educational field can bring them into the public sphere. It can enlarge their vision and widen their outlook. Education plays a major role in molding the behaviour and personality development of women. 53.7 per cent of the respondents were engaged in social service activities to some extent and 28.7 per cent of them did not involve in such activities at all. A lower level of participation in social services is a negative indicator of social empowerment.

Table 4.18: Educational status and social service activities

Educational Status	Social Service Activities				χ^2	df	p-value
	To a Great Extent (%)	To Some Extent (%)	Not at all (%)	Total			
Illiterate	6 (10.7)	24 (42.9)	26 (46.4)	56	71.046**	6	0.005
Primary	15 (8.4)	112 (62.6)	52 (29.1)	179			
Pre-degree	21 (47.7)	21 (47.7)	2 (4.5)	44			
Graduate	11 (52.4)	4 (19.0)	6 (28.6)	21			
Total	53 (17.7)	161 (53.7)	86 (28.7)	300			

** Significant at 1% level ($p<0.01$)

Respondents with higher education had found some way of representation in these social service groups and its activity. About 62.2 per cent of the primary educated said that they had participation only to some extent. The table clearly shows that most of the illiterates did not have any participation in social work activities. Even though education equips them to participate in social work activities, they get limited opportunity to do so.

The χ^2 value calculated for 6 degrees of freedom is 71.046 for the corresponding p-value of 0.005. Hence we reject the null hypothesis; making it is clear that the educational status of the SC women and their involvement in the social activities are significantly related.

Age at Marriage and Social Service Activities

In terms of social participation, age at marriage plays an important role. In most of the socio-cultural activities of the women ardent interest and zeal are playing a crucial role.

Table 4.19: Age at marriage and involvement in social service activities

Age at Marriage	Social Service Activities				χ^2	df	p-value
	To a Great Extent (%)	To some Extent (%)	Not at all (%)	Total			
Below 18 years	5 (10.6)	19 (40.4)	23 (48.9)	47			
18-21	13 (10.0)	89 (68.5)	28 (21.5)	130	33.025**	4	0.005
22 Above	33 (29.7)	48 (43.2)	30 (27.0)	111			
Total	51 (17.7)	156 (54.2)	81 (28.1)	288			

** Significant at 1% level (p<0.01)

Active women from SHGs have been elected to public offices, social service organizations etc. Their participation in such groups has been instrumental in empowering them. The 18-21age category had maximum participation in SHGs and social service activities. The same expanded their knowledge about social activities and its importance. So, when these women were given a chance to work with a social group, they tried to utilize it. About 68.5 per cent of them said that, they took part in social service activities. The representation was less among the lower and higher age groups. Only 5 per cent in the age group below 18 years said that their participation in social service activity was to a great extent.

The χ^2 value calculated for 4 degrees of freedom is 33.025 for corresponding p-value of 0.005. Hence, we reject the null hypothesis. Making it clear that, the age at marriage among SC women and their involvement in the social activity were significantly related.

Occupation and Social Service Activities

Occupation is one of the important indicators of women empowerment. It is generally assumed that occupation improves the socio-economic status of women. Many studies reveal that employment opportunities can change the attitudes and status of SC women. Women participation in social work makes them independent which is likely to build strong social relation of the women. It paves way for their social liberation.

Occupation is an important ingredient in moulding participation. Due to marriages or by association women migrate along with their husbands, which affect the occupational pattern of both the parties, which have an indirect implication in political participation in the locality.

Women today have won more independence and freedom of action than ever before. Women have successfully challenged the inequality in finding occupation to secure their livelihoods. Even though they have less control over income and assets, they have started to work and provide their share in family welfare. Most of the respondents who are labourers have shown more interest in participating in social work activities. About 50.9

percent said that they took part in social work activities to some extent. This particularly takes place in the space provided by the Gramasabhas/SHGs/NHGs. But their involvement is limited when it comes to dedicated social work. All groups have fewer participants when it comes to fulltime social work activities. The self employed find more time for participation due to their job nature which permits them to find more free time which can be utilized for social work. About 65.2 percent participated to some extent in social work activities. The table clearly indicates that the employed SC women also have shown more interest in social work activity.

Table 4.20: Occupation and social service activities

Occupation	Social Service Activity			Total	χ^2	df	p-value
	To a Great Extent (%)	To some Extent (%)	Not at all (%)				
Employed	23 (42.6)	18 (33.3)	13 (24.1)	54	32.298**	6	0.005
Self Employed	7 (15.2)	30 (65.2)	9 (19.6)	46			
Labour	13 (10.5)	73 (58.9)	38 (30.6)	124			
Unemployed	10 (13.2)	40 (52.6)	26 (34.2)	76			
Total	53 (17.7)	161 (53.7)	86 (28.7)	300			

** Significant at 1% level ($p<0.01$)

The χ^2 value calculated for 6 degrees of freedom was found to be 32.298 for the corresponding p-value of 0.005. Hence, we reject the null hypothesis. This suggests that the occupational status of the SC women and their involvement in the social activities are found to be significantly related.

Monthly Income and Social Service Activities

Women who enter into job market may have different reasons for social involvement. Economic need has been repeatedly cited as one of the most important factors of encouraging women to join work (Nath.1968, Gordon.1979). Women have been considered as secondary breadwinners in the family. If men's income is fair enough to manage the family, there is no need for women contribution, but if the dependent wages are low, one person's income may not be sufficient for the whole family (Sethi. 1976).

Table 4.21: Monthly income and involvement in social service activities

Monthly Income (Rs.)	Social Service Activities				χ^2	df	p-value
	To a Great Extent (%)	To some Extent (%)	Not at all (%)	Total			
501-1000	17 (10.8)	106 (67.1)	35 (22.2)	158	55.668**	4	0.005
1001-3000	16 (15.1)	47 (44.3)	40.6 (43)	106			
Above 3001	20 (55.6)	8 (22.2)	8 (22.2)	36			
Total	53 (17.7)	161 (53.7)	86 (28.1)	300			

** Significant at 1% level ($P<0.01$)

The table shows that among the respondents higher income group shows more participation in social service activities. About 55.6 per cent in the income group between 3001 and above show active participation in social service activities. This is because most of them are having regular monthly salary. They may be occupied in government service or well maintained private farms. Their occupation has given them the sense of self work, belief in their ability and confidence which have helped them to interact with social service organizations and participate in their activity. Respondents in the lower income group showed less participation and reported participation to some extent only. 40.6 per cent of the respondents in the income group 1001 3000 show no interest in social service activity. This is because they have to toil the whole day to earn his bread for the day and find less spare time to participate in the social work groups. Most of them do not like participate in social work activities sacrificing their bread.

The χ^2 value calculated for 4 degrees of freedom was found to be 55.668 for the corresponding p-value of 0.005. Hence, we reject the null hypothesis. It is clear that the monthly income of the SC women and their involvement in the social activities are significantly related variables. The ANOVA results also show a positive association of SC women's involvement in the social activities with the independent variables such as age, age at marriage, occupation and monthly income.

Conclusion

Social empowerment is a part of the whole process of empowerment. In this chapter various aspects of social empowerment with regard to decision making capacity before and after attending the government agencies programmes is analyzed. Before the participation in the government agencies over half of the respondents (54 %) rarely took decisions in their family and only 33.7 per cent often participated in the decision making process. The cross table analysis shows that the groups that fall under younger age, graduate level educated, higher age at marriage, the employed, and the high income exhibited a relatively higher decision making capacity before the participation in government programmes. After attending the programme, for 46.3 per cent of respondents, the decision making capacity improved to some extent. Further analysis with the variables reveals that the level of improvement in decision making capacity was relatively high among the younger age respondents, the educated, the respondents with higher age at marriage, that hail from the joint families, the employed and high income groups than their respective counter parts. Thus it can be concluded that socio-economic conditions do have greater role in empowering the SC women. The women who are placed better in the socio-economic ladder always had better chance for empowerment.

The preference for male child is an important negative indicator in the way of the empowerment process. More than three fourth of the respondents (78%) did not have any preference for a male child. Among the various significant variables, the highly educated respondents and the high income respondents did not prefer male children at all. Their equal concern for both male and female children is a positive indicator of empowerment.

85.3 per cent of respondents opined that they could travel without the male escorts. In this segment age, education and family type were found to be the significant variables having a role in the freedom of mobility of SC women. Similarly participation in social work was observed to have increased to some extent for more than half of the respondents (53.7 %). Among the statistically significant variables, the younger age, age at marriage, the employment status and income of the respondents moderated social service activities of the respondents.

5

Economic Empowerment of Scheduled Caste Women

Economic empowerment implies the development of the means to earn an income sufficient to lead a dignified life and satisfy the requisites of food, shelter and clothing. One of the most essential features of development is the transformation of society, which embraces the movement from traditional relations, social norms, health care, education and methods of production to more modern ones. Most societies demonstrate a blend of the old (traditional) and the new (modern) features. However, the transition from the old to new is not an end in itself, rather only a means towards the end. The changes associated with development provide societies as well as individuals more control and influence over their own destiny. Development enriches the lives of individuals by widening the horizon of choices and freedoms by way of eliminating their sense of isolation. Hence, the development strategy must aim at facilitating the transformation of society by identifying the potential catalysts and barriers to change.

The experience over the last five decades has demonstrated that there is always a potential to develop but it is not always visible. It is seen that while few countries succeed in achieving rapid economic growth and poverty alleviation, others are not so successful. The rapid growth of most of the East Asian economies shows that successful development could be accompanied by poverty reduction, widespread improvements in living standards and democratization. The policies of liberalization, privatization and globalization opened up a new phase of development.

Although, the development priorities differ from country to country, some common elements could be seen. The most important among them is education, as in its absence a country cannot develop i.e. cannot attract and build modern industries and cannot adopt innovative technologies in the rural sector. Education enables people to learn, acquire values and standards of behaviour, and also accept and transform gender roles. A basic health standard should be viewed as a fundamental human right and the strategies to upgrade the health standard must form an integral part of any holistic development strategy. Knowledge and education enriches human spirit and a more productive society can be ensured only by an educated and healthy community. The power of Knowledge is enormous; it multiplies the magnitude of the output that can be produced with the limited resources. The Capacity building of individuals is a sine-qua-none of empowerment for social transformation, economic development, participation in development process and representation in governance. Hence a country aspiring to develop must have institutions, entrepreneurship and leadership to catalyses, absorb and manage the process of change. The 1990s was a decade that belonged to democratic forces, participatory decentralized rural development, civil societies and human development (Subrahmanyam, 2003).

Rural development is conceptualized as a process of improving the living standards of the masses of low income categories residing in rural areas and making the process of their development self - sustaining (Lele, 1975). In developing countries rural development has become a distinct approach and strategy implemented mainly by the Government, NGOs and private agencies. It encompasses multi-sectoral components and is broader in its approach. It requires an interdisciplinary approach. Its focus on poverty, inequality and distributive justice and makes it focus on a special category of interventions for bringing about socio-economic change (World Bank, 1997).

In the 1950s the United Nations identified community development as 'synonymous with community participation' (Moser, 1989). Community development was seen as a process designed to create conditions of economic and social progress for the entire community with the active participation of its members. The core elements of community development are: (i) participation of the people in local projects; (ii) democratic decentralization; (iii) transfer of technology; and (iv) self-help efforts. In India, Government initiated community development movement in 1952, which underwent rapid changes during the last decades and current focus is on the decentralisation and empowerment of weaker sections.

The local self governing bodies are acting as the effective agencies for empowering the different segments of the society. Empowerment is a social process which has different dimensions and the following segment focuses on the economic empowerment.

Change in the Income Levels

Home based-work is a major area where several women are engaged. They turn into such kind of works for a number of reasons. Lack of necessary qualifications and formal training, absence of childcare support, social & cultural constraints and absence of alternatives are some of the reasons. Home-based worker belongs to the general category of workers who carry out remunerative work within the premises of their homes or in its surroundings. Inability to secure formal employment and reduced returns from agriculture, often force men to migrate to urban centres, leaving behind women and children (Annapurna, 2003). As home-based work being the only alternative available to the poorest communities, it is not just confined to women alone but involves children, especially girls. There are some positive aspects to home-based work. It enables women to combine work with domestic chores in flexible and sometimes better working conditions. While framing strategies to meet the challenges, it is important to uphold the positive aspects of home-based work. It is to be acknowledged that majority of women regularly wake up before dawn in order to ensure a better life for themselves and their families. (Grimes, 2000)

It is rightly observed that the economic empowerment of SC women is very essential for improving their position in the society. It is also pointed out that women's employment would lead not only to their self-development but also of their families. However, from the very beginning, women in India lagged far behind men in terms of employment. Traditionally, women in India economically depended upon their families and this dependency syndrome still continues to prevail.

The following table analyses the role of government sponsored agencies in improving the income levels of SC women. Among the 300 respondents, 29 respondents (9.7 %) from all age groups said that their income have raised greatly, for 102 respondents (34%) their income raised fairly, for 162 respondents (54%) income remained the same and for 7 respondents (2.3%) their income decreased.

Age and Change in the Income Levels

The important implementing agencies of democratic decentralization at the local levels are Gramasabha, NHGs, and SHGs. As these groups are structurally formed to cater the marginalized people such, the deprived sections of society like SC women get entry into these groups. Such groups create opportunities for income generation activities that enhance the quality of life of* families.

Table 5.1 shows that 13.4 per cent of the sample respondents in the age group of 34-41 years were of the opinion that joining the SHGs have enabled them to improve their income levels to a great extent. The respondents in the age group of 42 years and above (11.8%) have also benefited from becoming members of SHG's.

Table 5.1: Age and change in the income levels

Age	Change in the Income Level					χ^2	df	p-value
	Great Increase	Fair Increase	Remains the same	Decreased	Total			
18-25	3 (6.1)	25 (51)	21 (42.9)	–	49	18.517*	9	0.030
26-33	6 (6.5)	23 (24.7)	61 (65.6)	3 (3.2)	93			
34-41	11 (13.4)	32 (39)	36 (43.9)	3 (3.7)	82			
42 Above	9 (11.8)	22 (28.9)	44 (57.9)	1 (1.3)	76			
Total	29 (9.7)	102 (34)	162 (54)	7 (2.3)	300			

* Significant at 5% level ($p<0.05$)

39 per cent of the respondents in the 34-41 age group showed that their income levels had improved fairly. The 42 and above age group claimed fair improvement (28.9%) in their income levels. For the majority of the respondents in the age group of 26-33 years (65.6%) there was no change in their income levels even after joining the SHGs. The persons belonging to the age group of 42 years and above also expressed that their income levels remained the same (57.9%).

In most of the SC families, women are doomed to be the sole bread winners. They fail to invest their time effectively as they are laden with the responsibility their families resulting in reduced frequency of their participation in the SHGs. The younger age group respondents (51%) were of the opinion that their income has fairly increased after joining the SHGs, while 42.9 percent said that their income remained the same. It is clear from the above table that, it is the youngsters who were able to gain economically the benefit. The peculiarity of age, desire to be independent, aspiration for better future, all force them to join the SHGs, undertake enterprise that result in change in their income levels. The χ^2 value calculated for 9 degrees of freedom is 18.517 with a p-value of 0.030. Hence we reject the null hypothesis. We can conclude that the relationship between the variables namely age and the income level is strongly significant.

Education and Change in the Income Levels

Education as an instrument of socialization is considered as a powerful catalytic agent of social change. This is the most effective agent for the improvement of the socio-economic conditions of the SCs, removal of their disabilities and acceleration of their integration process. Framers of the Constitution realized the importance of education and have included in the Directive Principles of State Policy the provisions for free and compulsory education for all children up to the age of 14 years and for promotion with special care in the educational and economic interests of the weaker sections, particularly the Scheduled Castes and Scheduled Tribes and protecting them from social injustice and all forms of exploitation. Article 15 (4) enables the State to make special provisions for the advancement of any socially and educationally backward class of citizens or for the SCs/ STs. Education is one of the crucial factors in the process of empowerment which can lead to awareness building of SC women in generating employment avenues.

Education is like the air we breathe; in every walk of our life we are in need it. When woman has education she can contribute something productive to the society. Aparna Mitra (2008) adds that, literacy is considered to be a powerful tool in determining the position of women in any society. Literacy leads to social, cultural and economic development. Additionally it gives women more autonomy and freedom.

Table 5.2: Education and Change in Income Levels

Education	Change in Income Level					χ^2	df	p-value
	Greatly Increased	Fairly Increased	Remained the same	Decreased	Total			
Illiterate	3 (5.4)	22 (39.3)	30 (53.6)	1 (1.8)	56			
Primary	23 (12.8)	41 (22.9)	109 (60.9)	6 (3.4)	179			
Pre degree	–	21 (47.7)	23 (52.3)	–	44	48.892**	9	0.005
Graduate	3 (14.3)	18 (85.7)	–	–	21			
Total	29 (9.7)	102 (34)	162 (54)	7 (2.3)	300			

** Significant at 1% level ($p<0.01$)

Table 5.2 projects the relationship between the education level of the respondents and their income after joining the SHGs. 60.9 per cent of the primary educated and 53.6 per cent of illiterate participants expressed that their income levels remained the same even after joining the SHGs. In contrast to this, 85.7 per cent of the graduate respondents and 47.7% of those who have completed pre-degree level among the sample pointed out that their income levels increased fairly and for 14.3 per cent of the graduate respondents even greatly. Only 12.8 per cent among the primary educated respondents could improve their income levels substantially through participation in the SHGs/NHGs.

The above analysis clearly indicates the role of education in improving the income levels. The women participants who had undergone the basic education expressed that they felt to be in a more advantageous position than that those women who did not have any formal education. As education helps in improving the involvement capacity of women, they were easily accepted as part of the groups like SHGs and NHGs.

The level of education is likely to have an impact on awareness in joining the SHGs to earn more income. The table indicates that 14.3 per cent of respondents with graduate level education reported that they were aware of the SHGs and joined the SHGs and their income also increased substantially. It is only 12.8 per cent of the primary educated respondents who could improve their income substantially. In the case of illiterate respondents the situation is even worse with just 5.4 per cent. 85.7 per cent of graduated respondents felt that their income have increased fairly after joining the SHGs and it was only 22.9 per cent among the respondents with primary education as their awareness level was much low.

The respondents other than the graduate category reported that their income levels remained the same as it was before joining the SHGs. This clearly indicates that mere participation in the SHGs is not a sufficient condition for economic betterment of SC women, but education matters to a great deal. The calculated value of χ^2 for 9 degree of freedom is found to be 48.892, for a corresponding p- value of 0.005, thereby forces to reject the null hypothesis. Hence, it may be concluded that there is significant relationship between education and improvement in income levels.

Status of Family

The tradition bound Indian society is more concerned about the status of their living, the family culture, custom and so on. The people from so called 'good family status' never let female members of their family to go out of home for any means of necessity. The economic status of the family is determined mostly by the male members. But unfortunately the rural people in India are poor, employed in different fields from scavenging to government offices and many are unemployed. Hence the rural women are to toil hard in many ways to improve their family status economically by joining the SHGs, NHGs, etc. Among the respondents 59.3 per cent opined that the status of their family improved to some extent and 39.7 per cent of them said that the status did not improved at all. One per cent of the respondents said that status of their families improved to great extent, because of their participation in various governmental programmes. Thus it can certainly be said that the empowerment level SC women is influenced by participation in these activities. This fact is furthers cross tabulated with significant independent variables as follows.

Age and Status in the Family

The status of women in the Pre-Independent era depended greatly on male members of the family. Male members were considered the bread winners of the family. The role of women was limited to assisting male members and doing household duties. Their mobility was curtailed by the stringent social norms and customs. The change from dependency to self-reliance was not an easy affair for women. In the case of SC women the condition was pathetic as they were considered an excluded category. SHGs and NHG create the avenues for employment generation. Involvement in these groups helps women to uplift their social life by improving their economic conditions. They are also accepted as bread winners of the family. Studies have shown that, education, marital status, family background and work status are the determining variables that affect women's occupational earnings and status attainment level. (Schuler Hashemi, 1994; Wydick, 2002; Ahmad, 2003; Schreiner and Wolle, 2003).

Table 5.3: Age and status in the family

Age	Status in the Family				χ^2	df	p-value
	To a Great Extent (%)	To some Extent (%)	Not at all (%)	Total			
18-25	–	34 (69.4)	15 (30.6)	49	14.050*	6	0.029
26-33	–	44 (47.3)	49 (52.7)	93			
34-41	1 (1.2)	49 (59.8)	32 (39.0)	82			
42 Above	2 (2.6)	51 (67.1)	23 (30.3)	76			
Total	3 (1.0)	178 (59.3)	119 (39.7)	300			

* Significant at % level ($p<0.05$)

In the table 5.4 it is observed that, the variables related to the presence of specific benefits from SHG membership are expected to reduce the potential for conflict. The regression confirms this notion to some extent. The grater the benefits the broader the incidence of conflict reduction (as for social unity, community, decision making, and marketing the benefits for temporary conflicts). The need for an evolution of groups over the life cycle perceives to be associated with participation in SHGs.

A very contradictory picture emerges from this table. The younger age group (18-25) as well as the elderly (42 and above) reported an improvement in their family status, while, the middle age respondents were not that optimistic about the role of participation in SHGs in changing their family status. Still about 59.8 per cent of the respondents in the age group of 34-41 and 47.3 per cent in the 26-33age group admit that the SHGs had changed their family status. Membership in SHGs means an added income, which in turn has raised the status of the family. The women, supplementing the family income, are made part of the decision making process in the family.

An adult member's status in the family mostly depends on his/her job. As unemployed adults, women are often seen as depending on the male members. Through employment generation activities, SHGs opens up a plethora of opportunities for women, especially the SC women. The perception about women changed drastically once they started to involve in self-employment activities. This helped to improve their confidence level making their involvement in the society more active and effective. The calculated value of χ^2 for 6 degrees of freedom is 14.050 for a corresponding p-value of

0.029. Hence we reject the null hypothesis. It may be concluded that the relationship between education and income levels is significant.

Family Type and Status in the Family

In the family structure, distinction is generally made between joint family and nuclear family. India has a specific place for her tradition, customs, culture etc. Most of these customs and traditions submerge and suppress SC women. In the name of culture and tradition women are still not allowed to break the chains. The following table shows the relationship between family type and improvement of status in their own families of the respondents. Change or improvement in the status of women in the family is seen by their involvement in the income generating activities.

Table 5.4: Family type and status in the family

Family Type	Improvement of Status in the Family				χ^2	df	p-value
	To a Great Extent (%)	To some Extent (%)	Not at all (%)	Total			
Joint family	2 (1.3)	77 (49.0)	78 (49.7)	157	14.452*	2	0.001
Nuclear family	1 (7)	101 (70.6)	41 (28.7)	143			
Total	3 (1.0)	178 (59.3)	119 (39.7)	300			

* Significant at % level ($p<0.05$)

The Table 5.5 reveals the position of respondents in their family. About 7 per cent of the respondents belonging to the nuclear family are of the opinion that their status in the family has improved after joining in the SHG's, while 1.3 per cent of the respondents of joint family said so. It is very clear that the empowerment is only in talk and not in actuality. Even the family members do not recognize her status in her own family and then how can she expect it from the society. SC men and family members too are tied to their tradition and culture with respect to their women folk.

70.6 per cent of the women members in the nuclear family expressed that the family's perception about them improved to some extent. 49 per cent of the respondents belonging to joint families also believed that their status in the family improved to some extent. At the same time 49.7 per cent of the respondents in the joint family type expressed that their status in the family remained the same.

By the development of the nuclear family system, the role of women in managing the family has increased. This prompted them to look for alternative avenues of employment such as SHGs. Self-employment was the better option for the women members since migration in search of jobs is not possible for women as they have to take care of other family members.

The calculated value of Chi- square for 2 degrees of freedom is 14.452, for a corresponding p- value of 0.001. Therefore, we can safely reject the null hypothesis and conclude that the relationship between the type of family and improvement in the status of the family is significant.

Savings

The savings in the family show very clearly that the economic development of the family improves its status in the society. Once, the family status goes down it is hard to regain. The savings in the life plays a very important role to maintain economic status. In the present study such an enquiry was made on the savings of S.C women respondents after joining in the SHGs, NHGs, etc. Many self-help programmes have incorporated elements of savings, which can be used for purposes such as health insurance and emergency loans, thereby serving as private safety nets.

31.3 per cent of the respondents opined positively that their economic status have improved to some extent. Only 4 per cent of the respondents said that their economic statuses have greatly increased. And for 52.7 per cent of respondents, economic status remained the same. Finally 12 per cent of the respondents have said that their status decreased after joining the SHGs and NHGs. This factor was further cross tabulated with significant variables such as age, education and income, etc.

Age and Savings

When we consider economic condition of SC women, savings from monthly income is an important criterion to evaluate their empowerment process. Most of the SC women work in the unorganised sector and their income pattern changes, according to the availability of work.

Table 5.5: Age and savings of the respondents

Age	Savings				Total	χ^2	df	p-value
	Great Increased	Fair Increased	Remained the same	Decreased				
18-25	–	23 (46.9)	17 (34.7)	9 (18.4)	49			
26-33	3 (3.2)	36 (38.7)	44 (47.3)	10 (10.8)	93			
34-41	2 (2.4)	23 (28)	42 (51.2)	15 (18.3)	82	38.509**	9	0.005
42 Above	7 (9.2)	12 (15.8)	55 (72.4)	2 (2.6)	76			
Total	12 (4)	94 (31.3)	158 (52.7)	36 (12)	300			

** Significant at 1% level ($p<0.01$)

It is shown in the table that 72.4 per cent of the respondents in the age group of 42 years and above expressed that their saving pattern remained more or less the same. But the respondents comprising the age group of 18-25 years said that their saving pattern fairly increased (46.9%). Only a small number of respondents in the age category of 42 years and above could increase their income to a great extent (9.2%).

The above analysis clearly indicates that the benefits and positive impacts of SHGs have not penetrated enough into the lives of SC women. One of the major reasons might be that the income pattern is unequally distributed and because of this they failed to invest their income for future purposes. The women working in the unorganized sector hardly earn for their daily sustenance. Most of the respondents never thought about savings for their future purposes. Major part of their income is spent on food, clothing and medicine. When lending and savings are concerned, one notes that with internal saving as well as lending conflict potential also increases even though with a negative coefficient on the amount saved per member. The higher amount of saving does actually have a very positive effect.

Here, in the table above, the age of the respondents is associated with their saving. This is the matter which we take into account. While considering status in society, it is to be noted that the fame will not give one status, rather it depends on the the economic background, especially, the savings you have in one's account. The respondents in the age group of 18-25 years reported that their savings is nil and 46.9 per cent of the respondents told that their savings have fairly increased, 34.7 per cent respondents in the same category told that their savings remained the same and 18.4 per cent of the respondents reckoned that their savings actually decreased.

3.2 per cent of respondents in the age group 26-33 years replied that their savings increased greatly, 38.7 percentages of respondents reported that their savings fairly increased, 47.3 per cent of sample respondents reported that their savings remained the same and for 10.8 per cent of the respondents, their savings decreased. 2.4 per cent of the respondents in the age group of 34-41years reported that their savings increased greatly, 28 per cent of the respondents reported that their savings fairly increased, for 51.2 percent of respondents savings remained the same and 18.3% of the respondents reported that their savings went down.

Finally, 9.2 % of the respondents in the age group of 42 years and above reported that their savings increased greatly, 15.8% reported that their savings had fairly increased, 72.4% were not satisfied with their savings because it was static and 2.6% reported that their savings diminished. It is obvious that the SC women's savings did not improve much in spite of their hard work. Even after joining the SHGs or NHGs their savings have not improved because of the debts they had accumulated before joining these groups. Many respondents from different age groups reported that their savings decreased because they are mundane to work hard, do not find time to spare and are not aware of these programs.

The calculated χ^2 value for 9 degrees of freedom is found to be 38.509, for a corresponding p-value of 0.000. Therefore by rejecting the null hypothesis, we conclude that, the relationship between the respondent's age and attaining financial autonomy (savings) is highly significant.

Education and Savings

Education will bring lot of conscientisation as Sangeetha Purushothaman (1998) shoots with the problems which are faced by poor rural women, that understanding the forms of organisations developed for these women requires knowledge of constraints under which women operate in countries like India, giving their positions in the economy and society their skills, needs and aspirations. This understanding necessitates flexible organisation. The use of credit and funds must be flexible and are equally important and their perceptions and realities should be validated as such. Today the educational institutions play a profound role in molding the personality of individuals. So an attempt is made to find out the relationship between education and savings of the respondents as depicted in the table below.

Table 5.6: Education and savings of the respondents

Education	Savings					χ^2	df	p-value
	Great Increased	Fair Increased	Remained the same	Decreased	Total			
Illiterate	2 (3.6)	10 (17.9)	43 (76.8)	1 (1.8)	56	60.447**	9	0.005
Primary	10 (5.6)	60 (33.5)	94 (52.5)	15 (8.4)	179			
Pre degree	–	20 (45.5)	15 (34.1)	9 (20.5)	44			
Graduate	–	4 (19)	6 (28.6)	11 (52.4)	21			
Total	12 (4)	94 (31.3)	158 (52.7)	36 (12)	300			

** Significant at 1% level ($p<0.01$)

With regard to education and saving pattern, 45.5 percent of respondents who have completed pre-degree level of education expressed that their savings had increased fairly. Same was true with the respondents who have primary level education. But 76.8 percent of illiterate respondents pointed out that their savings remained more or less the same. It clearly shows that education plays a vital role in improving savings.

The calculated χ^2 for 9 degrees of freedom is 60.447, for a corresponding p-value of 0.005. Therefore we reject the null hypothesis and conclude that, the relationship between the respondent's education and financial autonomy is highly significant.

Family Type and Savings

The family type of the respondents influence the attitude towards savings as well as the skills imbibed through the programs to generate money. The relationship between the savings and the family type of the respondents is given in the table below.

Table 5.7: Family type and savings of the respondents

Family Type	Savings					χ^2	df	p-value
	Great Increased	Fair Increased	Remained the same	Decreased	Total			
Joint family	3 (1.9)	40 (25.5)	86 (54.8)	28 (17.)	157			
Nuclear family	9 (6.3)	54 (37.8)	72 (50.3)	8 (5.6)	143	16.820**	3	0.001
Total	12 (4)	94 (31.3)	158 (52.7)	36 (12)	300			

* Significant at % level ($p<0.05$)

From the total of 157 joint families, fir 1.9 per cent savings has increased greatly as against 6.3% of nuclear families. Here, it can be observed that as compared to joint family, nuclear family shows increase in savings. While 25.5 per cent of the respondents living in joint families were able to make savings out of the income, about 37.8 per cent living in nuclear family were able to do so.

In the matter of savings it is clearer that the joint family is not able to save their earnings like nuclear family because joint families are more flexible and their earning is less, they have to take care of the needs of their children, in- laws and aged dependents, and lack of time to work, participate and not aware of these programs. Even though nuclear family is having some savings; only 6.3% of them reported that their savings have been increased. There must emerge a drastic change among the SC women to earn more and save it for future. The calculated χ^2 value for 3 degrees of freedom is 16.820, for a corresponding p-value of 0.001. Therefore we reject the null hypothesis concluding that, there is a significant relationship between the family type and the attainment of financial autonomy (savings).

At the time of independence, scheduled castes were mostly engaged in jobs, which were considered to be too menial to be performed by other castes. They were mainly employed as agricultural workers, tanners, flayers and the like in the lower rungs of the society. Since then, supported by the various programmes, the SCs have been able to make slow but steady progress economically though not at par with the general population. Despite the progress achieved, there has been no significant shift in employment pattern among them. Primary sector in 1991 employed 77.11 per cent of SC workforce representing a decrease of 2 per cent in a decade (1981-91). Progress was not fair, achieved only in the tertiary sector, where employment of SCs, were up from 10.78 per cent in 1981 to 13.06 per cent in 1991. In some cases, there has been a negative shift in important sectors. This has reflected in the decrease in the number of cultivators among SCs. The change may have occurred on account of several factors such as diversion of land for non-agricultural purposes, population growth, migration and sale of land by SCs. While 28.17 per cent of the SC workforce was cultivators in 1981, their percentage decreased to 25.44 per cent in 1991. During the same decade, there has been an increase in the percentage of SCs engaged as agricultural labourers. It rose from 48.22 per cent in 1981 to 49.06 percent in 1991. During 1993-94, about half of the SC workforce was found engaged as agricultural labourers while 19.12 per cent were self-employed in the agricultural sector. More than 60 percent rural SC workforce was reported as labourers. In the urban areas, about 40 percent SCs were engaged as regular wages/salaried workers, while above one-fourth of the work force was reported as self employed. Thus women's employment becomes crucially important in economically supporting the families with sufficient income and standard living conditions (Mirala, 1983).

Dalit women rarely own land and most of them work on daily wages, as agricultural labourers. In rural India in 1991 around 71 % of Dalit women workers were engaged in farming, only less number of people were cultivators. The recent national survey shows that the unemployment rate among Dalit women on current daily basis is 4 %, while it is 9% for non-SC/ST women.

Occupation and Savings

Women's status is determined by many factors that determine the level of her economic dependence on men. Even though, women work harder and longer hours in most of the countries, their contribution is marginalized. This reflects the reproduction of patriarchal ideologies regarding women's work and place which is a key factor in the transmission of low female status (Archana Patkar, 1995). As earning is the main source of livelihood, women's employment has become crucially important in the economic support of families with insufficient incomes and substandard living conditions (Mirala, 1983). An attempt is made to bring out the relationship between occupation and the savings of the respondents in the table below.

Table 5.8: Occupation and savings of the respondents

Occupation	Savings					χ^2	df	p-value
	Greatly Increased	Fairly Increased	Remained the same	Decreased	Total			
Employed	–	18 (33.3)	15 (27.8)	21 (38.9)	54			
Self employed	6 (13)	12 (26.1)	24 (52.2)	4 (8.7)	46			
Labour	6 (4.8)	26 (21)	85 (68.5)	7 (5.6)	124	81.201**	9	0.005
Unemployed	–	38 (50)	34 (44.7)	4 (5.3)	76			
Total	12 (4)	94 (31.3)	158 (52.7)	36 (12)	300			

** Significant at 1% level (p<0.01)

Table 5.9 points out the savings of the sample respondents with respect to the type of their occupation after joining the SHGs. The condition is more pathetic when we view their savings, because the employed respondents have no savings. 33.3 per cent of the respondents reported that their savings had fairly increased, while 27.8 per cent of respondents felt it was stagnant and 38.9 per cent of the respondents' savings had further decreased. Among the self-employed respondents, 13 per cent reported that their savings had increased greatly and for 52.2 per cent it remained the same and in the case of 8.7 per cent respondents their savings decreased.

When the labourers' monthly income and savings were scanned, for the 68.5% savings remained the same, 4.8 per cent of them reported that their savings got increased greatly and 5.6 % respondent's savings decelerated. The calculated χ^2 value for 9 degrees of freedom is 81.201, with a corresponding p-value of 0.000. Therefore by rejecting the null hypothesis we conclude that, the relationship between the respondents occupation and attaining financial autonomy is highly significant.

Monthly Income and Savings

Achievement of financial autonomy is an indicator of women's economic empowerment. After earning an income and participating in income generating activities women gradually learn to handle money and related affairs. Thus women gain expertise in financial management and will become more autonomous. In the present study an attempt is made to find out the relationship between SC women's monthly income and their savings and the findings is presented in the table below.

Table 5.9: Monthly income and savings of the respondents

Monthly Income (Rs.)	Savings					χ^2	df	p-value
	Great Increased	Fair Increased	Remained the same	Decreased	Total			
501-1000	7 (4.4)	55 (34.8)	86 (54.4)	10 (6.3)	158	83.567**	6	0.005
1001-3000	3 (2.8)	37 (34.9)	61 (57.5)	5 (4.7)	106			
3001 Above	2 (5.6)	2 (5.6)	11 (30.6)	21 (58.3)	36			
Total	12 (4)	94 (31.3)	158 (52.7)	36 (12)	300			

** Significant at 1% level ($p<0.01$)

Analysis of monthly income and the saving pattern of the respondents reveal that for 34.9 per cent of respondents who earn their monthly income in the range of Rupees 1001-3000, the savings had fairly increased. The respondents who earn their monthly income between Rupees 501-1000 also revealed a fair increase in their savings. But the majority of respondents (57.5%), who earned their monthly salary in the range of 1001-3000 Rupees, expressed that their savings remained more or less the same. Only a small number of respondents, who have the monthly salary above 3001 Rupees, showed a substantial increase in their savings (5.6%).

It could be seen that 58.3 per cent of the respondents earn their monthly income in the range of Rs. 3001 and above. Usually these monthly income earners necessities are more and are greedy to develop their house with luxurious gadgets without effective income. So they approach money lenders when they are in need and pay the debts when they get their wages. This adversely affects their saving habits.

The calculated χ^2 value for 6 degrees of freedom is 86.567, with a corresponding p-value of 0.005. Therefore we safely rejecting the null hypothesis and conclude that, the relationship between the respondent's monthly income and attaining financial autonomy is highly significant.

Control over Income

Women after joining the SHGs and NHGs become aware of the amount of money the whole household is bringing in; consequently there is the possibility that women demand a certain amount to be kept for specific purposes, whether for hospital care, schooling for children and the like. This development is an improvement in the situation for women. Women's loans easily get diverted in enhancing household assets and incomes but do not ensure her co-ownership of the family's productive assets. Thus access to credit need not necessarily result in her empowerment. In such situations, the household may benefit but the woman herself is likely to be further deepening of the resource division between herself and her husband (Garikipati.S, 2008).

Allegedly, the women spend more money on individual consumption, such as bangles, health care and ornaments, as well as sending their children and daughters to private institutions. Women in the groups are gradually taking more decision's regarding the purchase of livestock in order to increase the resources of the family; the cattle they purchase are registered in their names. Since the female members in the family earn their living to feed everyone in her family, she can have the control over the income. 97 (32.3%) out of the 300 respondents take control over their income to a great extent, 149 respondents (49.7%) control have over their income to some extent, 54 respondents (9.18%) seldom take control over their income. An analysis is made to know the respondents control over their income with respect to their age, education, family type, etc.

Age and Control over income

Age is both a biological and social phenomena. Socially a person's age denotes the person's capacity to fulfill his socially assigned roles. Having income security, possession of ownership of productive assets and developing entrepreneurship skills are the important assets of economic empowerment. It would provide information for improving their capacity for productivity and would help women to attain income security (James Antony 2004). An analysis is made to know the respondents' control over their income in the table below.

Table 5.10: Age and control over income

Age	Control over Income				χ^2	df	p-value
	To a Great Extent (%)	To some Extent (%)	Not at all (%)	Total			
18-25	24 (49)	24 (49)	1 (2)	49	22.758**	6	0.001
26-33	27 (29)	41 (44.1)	25 (26.9)	93			
34-41	28 (34.1)	45 (54.9)	9 (11)	82			
42 Above	18 (23.7)	39 (51.3)	19 (25)	76			
Total	97 (32.3)	149 (49.7)	54 918)	300			

* Significant at 1% level ($p<0.01$)

With regard to the control over one's own income the above table mentions that 54.9 per cent of respondents under the age group of 34-41 years expressed that they had control over their income up to some extent. 34.1 per cent of respondents in the same age category revealed that they had greater control over their income. 51.3 per cent of respondents under the age group of 42 years and above also said that they had control over their own income up to some extent. This pattern clearly indicates that age and responsibility positively correlated and that with advancement in age there is a natural tendency to have control over one's own income.

By analyzing the table, it is found that 26.9 per cent of the respondents belong to 26-33 age category have no control over their own income. 25 per cent of the respondents in the age group category of 42 years and above also told the same. 49 per cent of the respondents in the age group category of 18-25 years reckoned that they had control over their own income to a great and some extent.

The calculated χ^2 value for 6 degrees of freedom is 22.758, for a corresponding p-value of 0.001. Therefore we reject the null hypothesis concluding that, the relationship between the age of the respondents and control over their own income is highly significant.

Education and Control over Income

Illiteracy has been a major setback, hindering women in their dealings with others. The traditional socio-economic factors like controlling of property ownership widen the gender gap in its utilization (Roy, K. Chaudhuri, 2008). Studies suggest that increased income under women's control has a positive impact on children's welfare (Tripp, 1981; Mencher, 1988). These studies conclude that women devote more of their incomes than men to the household's daily subsistence and nutrition (Jaquette, 1993). The data collected on the educational level of the respondents and control over their income is presented in the table below.

Table 5.11: Education and Control over income

Education	Control Over Income				χ^2	df	p-value
	To a Great Extent (%)	To some Extent (%)	Not at all (%)	Total			
Illiterate	18 (32.1)	25 (44.6)	13 (23.2)	56	42.530**	6	0.001
Primary	71 (39.7)	69 (38.5)	39 (21.8)	179			
Pre degree	6 (13.6)	36 (81.8)	2 (4.5)	44			
Graduate	2 (9.5)	19 (90.5)	–	21			
Total	97 (32.3)	149 (49.7)	54 (18)	300			

** Significant at 1% level (p<0.01)

When analysed the education and control over one's own income, the above table shows that 90.5 per cent of graduate respondents felt that they had control over their income up to some extent. 81.8 per cent of the respondents, who have the educational background up to pre-degree level also expressed that they had control over their income to some extent. This trend clearly shows that with higher education, the respondents show greater sense of responsibility and understanding about their income and expenditure.

While 99 per cent of the graduates were able to control their income, the number gradually decreases with those with less in education. Attitudes of women change with education, with higher education, she is able to acquire a job and make independent decisions. Being an earning members of the family, she is able to control her income. With less education, women usually acquire jobs of low status which in turn force her to be under men in all respects. The education is the liberalizing force for SC women from the clutches of the patriarchal society.

The calculated χ^2 value for 6 degrees of freedom is 42.530, for a corresponding p-value of 0.000. Therefore by rejecting the null hypothesis we conclude that the relationship between the respondents' educations and their ability to gain control over their own income is highly significant.

Family Type and Control over Income

Strong patriarchal systems and the resulting attitudinal bias play a major role in determining subjective education and related decisions. In a traditional society like ours the family has a greater say in all her movements like thinking and implementing it. A study is conducted to understand the relation of the SC women's control over the income she earned with their family type and the result is given in the table below.

Table 5.12: Family type and control over income

Family Type	Control over Income				χ^2	df	p-value
	To a Great Extent (%)	To some Extent (%)	Not at all (%)	Total			
Joint family	35 (22.3)	88 (56.1)	34 (21.7)	157			
Nuclear family	62 (43.4)	61 (42.7)	20 (14)	143	15.418**	2	0.005
Total	97 (32.3)	149 (49.7)	54 918)	300			

** Significant at 1% level (p<0.01)

It is seen that 56.1 per cent of respondents belonging to joint family had control over their own income to some extent. 42.7 per cent of respondents who belongs to nuclear family expressed that they had control of their own income to some extent. At the same time, 43.4 per cent of respondents belonging to the nuclear family exercise greater control over their own income. But 21.7 per cent of the joint family respondents and 14 % of the nuclear family respondents not have necessary control over their own income.

The basic reason why the SC woman not possessing control over her own income is that her husband and family members are not ready to accept her, they don't like her to take decisions of her own, they want her to be under the feet of men. The subhuman attitudes of males towards the SC women are accepted by the society. In the absence of sufficient income of her own, a woman will not be in a position to something that she thinks necessary for the household. The society should change its outlook and accept women as just like men.

The calculated χ^2 value for 2 degrees of freedom is 15.418, for a corresponding p-value of 0.005. Therefore we reject the null hypothesis and conclude that the relationship between the respondent's family type and control over their own income is highly significant.

Occupation and Control over Income

As most SC women, have to depend on the wages from manual labour to earn their living, they have a poor economic base and higher unemployment rate. This is seen in terms of their low standard and high level poverty. Poverty levels are quite high among the farmers and casual labourers. Naturally, this leads them to have sub-standard housing and other basic amenities. In many rural societies, a woman is considered an economic asset and considerable value is placed on a hard-working, industrious and dutiful wife (Chudhuri, 1978).

Table 5.13: Occupation and control over income

Occupation	Control over Income				χ^2	df	p-value
	To a Great Extent (%)	To some Extent (%)	Not at all (%)	Total			
Employed	12 (22.2)	39 (72.2)	3 (5.6)	54	35.357**	6	0.001
Self Employed	13 (28.3)	28 (60.9)	5 (10.9)	46			
Labour	52 (41.9)	38 (30.6)	34 (27.4)	124			
Unemployed	20 (26.3)	44 (57.9)	12 (15.8)	76			
Total	97 (32.3)	149 (49.7)	54 (18)	300			

** Significant at 1% level ($p<0.01$)

In the table the variables considered are occupation of the respondents against the control over their own income. 41.9 per cent of labour respondents had control of their own income, 28.3 per cent of the self employed, 26.3 per cent of the unemployed and the 22.2 per cent of the employed respondents enjoyed control on their own income to a great extent.

The higher income groups have a better stake over their income compared to those who earn low incomes. 72.2 per cent of the employed respondents have a say over their income to some extent. Unemployed women often depend on the male bread winner. The long years of dependence, subjugation and exploitation have forced these women to come out, gain employment and liberate themselves from the male domination. The calculated χ^2 value for 9 degrees of freedom is 35.357, for a corresponding p-value of 0.000. Therefore we reject the null hypothesis and conclude that the relationship between the respondents' occupation and attaining control over their own income is highly significant.

Monthly Income and Control over Income

Collective actions through the SHGs help women to break out of the gender and economic barriers, and enabled them to expand their horizons for their own development as individuals, family, group and community. Here, an attempt is made to bring out the relationship between the monthly income of the respondents and their ability to control their income and the result is given in the table below. Including the variable that measures the extent to which household expenditure depends on women earnings, on the grounds that women are likely to have greater access and control over resources if they are the primary earners in a household (Sunita Kishore and Kamla Gupta 2004).

Table 5.14: Monthly income and control over income

Monthly Income	Control over Income				χ^2	df	p-value
	To a Great Extent (%)	To some Extent (%)	Not at all (%)	Total			
501-1000	74 (46.8)	72 (45.6)	12 (7.6)	158	60.475**	4	0.005
1001-3000	18 (17)	49 (46.2)	39 (36.8)	106			
3001 Above	5 (13.9)	28 (77.8)	3 (8.3)	36			
Total	97 (32.3)	149 (49.7)	54 (18)	300			

** Significant at 1% level ($p<0.01$)

The table 5.15 displays the monthly income of the sample respondents and their positions in having control over their own income. The vast majority of the respondents accounting for 77.8 per cent with monthly income of Rs. 3001 and above reported that they had control over their own income to some extent. 8.3 per cent of them never exercised this control. 46.8 per cent of the respondents from 501-1000 monthly income category reported that they had greater control over their own income and 36.8 per cent of the respondents from the monthly income category of Rs. 1001-3000 had no control over their own income at all.

With regard to monthly income and control over one's own income, the above table indicates that 77.8 per cent of respondents with income of Rs.3001 and above could exercise control over their own income to some extent. The majority of the respondents who earn their monthly income in the range of Rs.501-1000 revealed that they had control over their own income either to some extent or to a great extent.

The χ^2 value calculated for 4 degrees of freedom is 60.475, for a corresponding p-value of 0.005. Therefore we reject the null hypothesis. Concluding that, the relationship between the respondents' monthly income and exercise of control over their income is highly significant.

Power to Dispose Assets

Power to dispose assets represents a means of economic independence. It serves to increase women's bargaining power and autonomy within the household and within society more broadly.

In the present study the disparities in the ownership of capital assets, employment, education and access to health services between the SCs and other households are considered. Although there has been some improvement in the ownership of capital assets, still a large proportion of SC households continue to depend on the traditional occupation of wage labour. Among the 300 respondents in the study, 55 (18.3%) exercised the right to dispose the assets to a great extent and 186 respondents (62 %) to some extent, while

59 respondents (19.7%) did not have any power to dispose the assets. A detailed study is made to know the power to dispose the assets and the findings are codified in the table below.

Age and Power to Dispose Assets

Usually age is a factor which creates a difference in thinking. The long and bitter life experiences of the elderly women prevent them from taking any such actions. To empower women literacy needs to be linked with livelihood issues from the very beginning. Rao (1993) tells in his study that a conscious effort to be initiated to provide women with literacy and skills. Women require training in a range of skills, such as managing assets and credit, handling local problems and conflict situations.

Table 5.15: Age and power to dispose of the assets

Age	Power to Dispose of the Assets				χ^2	df	p-value
	To a Great Extent (%)	To some Extent (%)	Not at all (%)	Total			
18-25	16 (32.7)	32 (65.3)	1 (2)	49	45.341**	6	0.005
26-33	12 (12.9)	62 (66.7)	19 (20.4)	93			
34-41	23 (8)	50 (61)	9 (11)	82			
42 Above	4 (5.3)	42 (55.3)	30 (39.5)	76			
Total	55(18.3)	186 (62)	59 (19.7)	300			

** Significant at 1% level ($p<0.01$)

Empowerment basically means transfer of power in which power is distributed equitably. Max Weber says that power is one's ability to influence decision making in public action affecting the community. So it is important to analyse the power of women to dispose of the assets acquired by them. In the above table, 66.7 per cent of respondents under the age group 26-33 years opined that they had the powers to dispose the assets which they have acquired themselves to some extent. 65.3 per cent of respondents under the age group of 18-25 also agreed with this. 32.7 per cent of respondents under the age group of 18-25 years expressed that they had greater powers to dispose the assets they have acquired. The process of empowerment is not a quantum jump. It is a very long process and in its way it has to face many failures, problems, and by trial and error it will be accepted finally by everyone.

Even the male members in the house are not ready to accept or allow women to do anything of their own. They escorting women all the way as if they doubt in the character of women.

The younger age groups have the freedom to dispose the assets as and when required, while the elders seen bit hesitant to do so. About the 80 per cent of the younger age group felt that after joining the SHGs they had got enough power to dispose the assets according to their wish, when 60 per cent of the elderly people felt that they too had acquired the same power. Among the respondents in the age group of 42 years and above, 5.3 per cent had credited that they had greater power to spend their assets, 55.3 per cent of the respondents reported that they had the power to dispose the assets only to some extent and 39.5 per cent of the respondents of the same age category accepted that they didn't have the power to spend what they have earned.

The above table clearly reveals the truth behind the powers of women in utilizing their own income. The 18-25 years age group respondents had the power to utilize their own income. They are able to exercise more powers than the elderly categories. The youngsters are bit different in thinking and determination, but the elderly people are not ready to give up the tradition and any power to the females. The χ^2 value calculated for 6 degrees of freedom is 45.341, for a corresponding p-value of 0.000. Therefore we reject the null hypothesis. We can conclude that, the relationship between the respondents' age and the power to dispose the assets they have acquired is highly significant.

Education and Power to Dispose Assets

In India, the socio-economic norms are crucial determinants of educational attainment of women. Women's status is a multidimensional concept referring to their access to and control over valued material and social resources and women's power of autonomy, i.e, their ability to control important events in their lives with freedom from control from others within the household (Cain *et al.*, 1979). The following table analyses whether SC women are having the power to dispose their assets in relation with level of education.

Table 5.16: Education and power to dispose of the assets

Education	Power to Dispose of the Assets				χ^2	df	p-value
	To a Great Extent (%)	To some Extent (%)	Not at all (%)	Total			
Illiterate	7 (12.5)	18 (32.1)	31 (55.4)	56	86.739**	6	0.005
Primary	21 (11.7)	133 (74.3)	25 (14)	179			
Pre degree	16 (36.4)	25 (56.8)	3 (6.8)	44			
Graduate	11 (52.4)	10 (47.6)	–	21			
Total	55 (18.3)	186 (62)	59 (19.7)	300			

** Significant at 1% level ($p<0.01$)

With regard to education and the power to dispose the assets that one have acquired, the table shows that majority of the respondents who had completed primary level education had powers to some extent to dispose of the assets (74.3%). But the illiterate respondents (55.4%) expressed that they did not have any control over their assets to dispose of. At the same time 52.4 per cent of graduate respondents pointed that they had greater control to dispose of the assets that they had acquired. Cent percent of the educationally graduated respondents recorded that they have all the power to dispose the assets they have earned either to some extent or to a great extent.

The calculated χ^2 value for 6 degrees of freedom is 86.739, for a corresponding p-value of 0.005. We therefore reject the null hypothesis. Hence, we can be conclude that the relationship between the respondents' education and the power to dispose the assets they have earned is highly significant.

Family Type and Power to Dispose Assets

Families in a militarized economy lead a very precarious life. Security for women and girls is at its nadir. The females were bound in the hands of males and survived inside the barrier, but now to help her family she must definitely come out. The family type and the power to dispose assets are studied in detail in the table below.

Table 5.17: Family type and power to dispose of the assets

Family Type	Power to Dispose Assets				χ^2	df	p-value
	To Great Extent (%)	To some Extent (%)	Not at all (%)	Total			
Joint family	34 (21.7)	86 (54.8)	37 (23.6)	157			
Nuclear family	21 (14.7)	100 (69.9)	22 (15.4)	143	7.303*	2	0.026
Total	55 (18.3)	186 (62)	59 (19.7)	300			

* Significant at 5% level ($p<0.05$)

The type of family is an important criterion to check whether the respondents are having powers to dispose of the assets that one has acquired. 69.9 per cent of nuclear family members expressed that they had powers to some extent. 23.6 per cent of respondents belonging to joint families expressed that they did not have any powers or control their assets.

Women hailing from nuclear families, with better economic status within the family are expected to demonstrate a higher percentage of power to dispose the assets they earned. But the above table shows that only 14.7 per cent of the respondents enjoy the power to dispose the assets they earned to a great extent, 15.4 per cent of the respondents from the same category accepted that they had no power at all.

When the joint family is concerned, they are traditional to the core not alone that they can spend a lot of their own due to burden of the family. The table reveals that 21.7 per cent of the respondents had the power to spend their own to a great extent, 54.8 per cent of the respondents reported that they had the power to some extent and 23.6 per cent of the respondents told that they didn't enjoy the power to dispose the assets they have earned.

It is evident that the family members still mind to keep in touch with the gender based violence, no power to women even to spend what she earned. The calculated χ^2 value for 2 degrees of freedom is found to be 7.303, for a corresponding p-value of 0.026. Therefore by rejecting the null hypothesis we can conclude that, the relationship between the respondents' family type and the power to dispose the assets one earned is highly significant.

Monthly Income and Power to Dispose Assets

The women struggle hard to earn even meager amount of income to save their family from hunger and provide for all the needs they want. When they struggle hard, they have to give away the assets they earned. Here in the table below a detailed study is conducted to learn the relation between monthly income of the respondents and the power to dispose the assets they earned.

Table 5.18: Monthly Income and power to dispose of the assets

Monthly Income (Rs.)	Power to Dispose of the Assets				χ^2	d f	p-value
	To a Great Extent (%)	To some Extent (%)	Not at all (%)	Total			
501-1000	28 (17.7)	101 (63.9)	29 (18.4)	158	44.085**	4	0.005
1001-3000	7 (6.6)	72(67.9)	27 (25.5)	106			
3001 Above	20 (55.6)	13 (36.1)	3 (8.3)	36			
Total	55 (18.3)	186 (62)	59 (19.7)	300			

** Significant at 1% level ($p<0.01$)

The above table shows that 67.9 per cent of respondents who earn their monthly income in the range of Rs.1001-3000 had powers to some extent to dispose of the assets that they have acquired. By analyzing the table it clear that 18.4 per cent of respondents who earn their monthly income in the range of Rs. 501-1000 said that they don't have any power to dispose the assets they had acquired, but 17.7 per cent of the respondents in the same category accepted that they had the power to dispose the assets.

Among the respondents with monthly income of Rs.3001 and above, 55.6 per cent feel that they have a great extent of power to dispose the assets which they have earned. 8.3 per cent of the respondents in the same category expressed that they did not have the power. Another 36.1 per cent of the respondents in the same category reported that they have the power to dispose the assets they have earned fairly well. 67.9 per cent of the respondents from the category of monthly income earners in the range of

Rs.1001-3000 exercise power to some extent to dispose the assets they have earned and only 6.6 per cent of the respondents from the same category have the absolute power to dispose the assets which they have earned.

From the table, it is understood very clearly that even though the SC women earn by themselves they are unable to use it for their sake. Still further, these women face many constraints from their own family and society and their empowerment still remains a serious questions. The calculated χ^2 value for 4 degrees of freedom is 44.085, for a corresponding p-value of 0.005. Therefore we reject the null hypothesis. Hence, we can conclude that, the relationship between the respondents' monthly income and the power to dispose the assets they have earned is highly significant.

Lending Loan

Earnings generated by taking loans have been instrumental in increasing the physical well-being of the household, often through better nutrition and sanitation. The household asset base is also been enhanced by the addition of jewelry (a portable asset), improved housing and land purchase in some cases. The large loans are an indication that these families have stable incomes that they are trusted in managing the repayments. In their meetings SHGs and NHGs women often reflect on their rights and economic progress and assess the ways in which these have meaning for their lives. In relation to the economy, women demand the right to avail loans and support for commercial activities. However, none of the women are contributing with the main income for their families in the rural areas. Supplementing the main income by their own means is more widespread among the women engaged in agriculture than those women with a share of a business and an income outside agriculture. Among the 300 respondents, 155 (51.7%) availed loans and 145 respondents (48.3%) did not go for it.

Occupation and Lending Loan

The economic status of the family needs to be analysed through an investigation of its members' occupation and income. In the present study women went for loans from money lenders, as they were not able meet the expenses of the family with the income they had. The table below shows the correlation between the occupation of the respondents and the money lent by them. Occasionally, as reported in the study of SHGs in Kerala, women members take loans for the benefit of others that include their husbands, brothers, sisters and parents (Sooryamoorthy, 2005b), and not necessarily for income generating activities. Marital status of women members therefore becomes a determinant in their loan use (Sooryamoorthy, 2005a).

Table 5.19: Occupation and availed of any loan from money lenders even after joining SHGs/NHGs

Occupation	Lending Loan			χ^2	df	p-value
	Yes (%)	No (%)	Total			
Employed	24 (44.4)	30 (55.6)	54	9.035**	3	0.029
Self Employed	32 (69.6)	14 (30.4)	46			
Labour	57 (46)	67 (54)	124			
Unemployed	42 (55.3)	34 (44.7)	76			
Total	155 (51.7)	145 (48.3)	300			

* Significant at 5% level (p<0.5)

The above table assesses whether the respondents availed loan from money lenders even after joining SHGs. 69.6 per cent of self employed respondents availed loans from money lenders, it may be mainly because their income level is not uniform and variations in the availability of work and initial investment. 54 per cent of respondents belonging to the category of casual labour did not receive any financial assistance from money lenders. Because nowadays the labours earn about Rs. 250/- per day and they control the expenses within their income limits. They send their children to the government schools or institutions where they can get stipend, and lead a very simple life. Khan (1999) also noted that, the married women spend their income on house hold utensils, good food, children's education and clothing. Women borrowers spend loans in a bid to increase their household income and to accumulate assets including; building houses, freeing land from mortgage or purchasing rickshaws. Potentially, women are more likely to make use of their income on household consumption and security related assets, while men borrowers spend it on productive activities (Kabeer1998).

The χ^2 value calculated for 3 degrees of freedom is 9. 035 for a corresponding p-value of 0.029. Therefore we reject the null hypothesis and conclude that, the relationship between the respondents' occupation and availing loan from money lenders even after joining the SHGs is highly significant.

Table 5.20: Monthly income and lending loan

Monthly Income (Rs.)	Lending Loan			χ^2	df	p-value
	Yes (%)	No (%)	Total			
501-1000	90(57)	68(43)	158	10.003**	2	0.007
1001-3000	55(51.9)	51(48.1)	106			
3001 Above	10(27.7)	26(72.2)	36			
Total	155(51.7)	145(48.3)	300			

** Significant at 1% level (p<0.05)

The table shows that 72.2 per cent of respondents who had monthly income in the range of Rs. 3001 and above did not avail loans from money lenders after joining SHGs/NHGs. But the respondents whose monthly income falls in the range of Rs. 501-1000 admitted that they have availed loans from moneylender, ie, 57 per cent of the respondents have availed loans from money lenders and the remaining 43 per cent of the respondents have reported that they did not get loans at all.

Among the monthly income earners ranging between Rs. 1001-3000, 51.9 per cent of the respondent's availed loan and 48.1 per cent of the respondents reported that they did not avail any loan from the money lenders. Of the monthly income category ranging from Rs. 3001 and above, 27.7 per cent of the respondents told that they are still behind money lenders even after joining the SHGs. But 72.2 per cent of the above category of respondents replied that they never went for loans from money lenders.

On the whole the money lenders play an important role in society by lending money with higher interest. Before the advent of SHGs these monthly income earners were lending money. The income they earned was not enough to meet their expenses and satisfy their needs. In most cases the debts they owe was outstanding from the period well ahead of their involvement with the SHGs activities. They are not able to come out of the debts they had before. One of the sample respondent told that, they are not willing to avail loans from money lenders as the later torture them physically and mentally. Further the interest is much higher compared to the scheduled banks.

The χ^2 value calculated for 2 degrees of freedom was 10.003, for a corresponding p-value of 0.007. Therefore we reject the null hypothesis and conclude that, the relationship between the respondents' monthly income and availing loan from the money lenders even after joining the SHGs is highly significant.

Conclusion

The Panchayati Raj system is acting as an effective agency in empowering the marginalized, especially the SC women. Empowerment is a multifarious social process having different dimensions. The level of empowerment taking place at the economic front has been analysed in this chapter. The level of change in the income had a mixed response among the respondents. For more than half of the respondents (54%) it remained the same, and only for 9.7 per cent it increased greatly, while for 34 per cent the income increased fairly. The cross table analysis shows that higher percentage of younger respondents, graduates, and higher income respondents improved their level of income after participation in the government programmes. The variables such as age, education, family type and income proved to be associated significantly with participation in the SHGs.

About 60 per cent of respondents opined that their status in the family improved to some extent. Even if it is not the optimum level, it is a positive indicator towards the process of empowerment. The cross-table analysis further showed that there exists a statistically significant association with the variables - age and family type - similarly with regard to savings also the analysis showed a mixed result. For half of them (52.7%), it remained the same and for 31.3 per cent, it increased fairly. The cross table analysis indicated that the variables such as age, education, family type, occupation and monthly income are statically associated with the dependent variable savings. It should be noted that the habit of saving was relatively higher among the younger age groups, moderately educated, members of nuclear family, unemployed and low income categories than their counterparts.

Control over income increased to some extent for half of the respondents (49.7 %) and for 32.3 per cent it increased to a great extent. The Chi-square test further showed that the independent variables such as age, education, family type, occupation and income have a statistically proven association with the control over income. Among the respondents higher level of control over income was exercised by the younger, educated, members of nuclear family, employed, and lower and higher income categories.

The power to dispose of assets had increased to some extend for 62 per cent of the respondents, and to a great extend for 18.3 per cent. The cross table analysis showed that the variables such as age, education, family type and income of SC women have positive association with their power to dispose of the assets acquired by them. Among the various categories, greater level of power to dispose the assets was found among the younger, the highly educated, and the respondents hailing from nuclear families.

The possibilities of approaching the money lenders even after attending the development programmes is a negative indicator in the process of empowerment. The analysis showed that over half of the respondents (51.7 %) still approach money lenders for availing loans. The cross table analysis showed that the independent variables such as occupation and monthly income are positively associated with the habit of availing loans.

Earning an income or making contributions to the family's welfare have a signaling effect of SC women's greater involvement in the making decisions on important issues within the household. Having access to an independent income is an important base for negotiation and building self-esteem.

6

Political Empowerment of Scheduled Caste Women

An important are were gender difference predominantly prevails is politics. Traditionally, politics has been considered to be the domain of the male folk. Until recently, women were not regarded as part of this most significant decision making process. In fact, this miserable lot were disinterested in such field because of their family responsibilities, economic dependency, inferior status and, most significantly, illiteracy.

Even though the nature of discrimination varies from one country to another, generally women are discriminated in this world in the social, economic and political spheres. Almost everywhere in the globe, men are looked as the principal decision makers, where as women hold a subordinate position in negotiations about family matters, political activity and so on. In fact, gender equality is a prerequisite for the effective participation of women in politics as their inferior position in political structures affects their ability to challenge the subordination in all its manifestations. But on the other side, there are many obstacles for the women participation in politics. An important obstacle that stand in the way of their full participation in politics is the social attitude that leads towards the subjugation of women, as their participation in politics, is closely connected to their marital status, family and employment. Today's prevailing political culture is a deterrent factor that destroys the life of women. Apart formthis the factor such as violence, character assassination and the ridiculous struggle for power very badly affect the active participation of women in politics.

It is a fact that there is no true governance and democracy that strive to ensure equal participation of men and women at different levels of decision making process. It is expected that women participation in politics will change the world by bringing new priorities and perspectives within the power structure. If women are to be empowered politically, the immediate imperative is to resort to different forms of affirmative action so that their voices are heard. If women are to be persons of their own right, they should possess the capacity to control of their own bodies and suitably find as empowered.

During the 19th century, India witnessed a wide range of social reform movements. As per Article 14, the constitution of India guarantees gender equality and protection of law by prohibiting discrimination on the ground of sex. Articles 23 and 42 have made provisions to provide for just and human conditions of work along with maternity reliefs. It is the constitutional duty of every citizen, as per Article 51A, to abstain from the derogatory practices against the dignity of women. In 1994, the Indian Parliament passed the 73rd Amendment to the Constitution which reserved one third of seats in the local self governments for women. This is a significant achievement towards the empowerment of women. Nearly one million women have come as decision makers at the Panchayat levels. Another significant effort to ensure reservation of 33% of seats in the Parliament and State Legislative Assemblies, the 81st amendment, remains in the shelves. It remains as a mirage in spite of the commitment affirmed by all political parties towards women empowerment (Lekshmi, S 2004).

Political empowerment is one of the most important aspects in the rating of women empowerment. This aspect of capacity building would enable women folk to make strong decisions. But, there are many socio-economic constraints that inhibit the effective participation of women in the politics as well as in the demographic institutional structures, force women to remain marginalized in the society.

Statistics, after the six decades of granting political equality, reveals that there is an acceptance visible manifestation of gender equality at the suffrage level, and power structure for women concern, but, according to the document on Women's Development in 1985, role of women politics virtually remained unchanged, despite the rapid growth of informal political activity (Biju M. R, 2009).

Basically, women candidates have to cross two hurdles before they enter into formal political structures. First, they should be nominees of parties which are the 'gatekeepers' of power; and second, they should be voter friendly. Due to the nexus of traditional status equations, the chances of women in politics have been highly limited. Moreover, the political parties do not favour the nomination of women candidates, as they are not sure of their success. Though all political parties do have a Women Wing, only very few women have access to the inner ring of the party, which is the core of power structure. Majority of women, being illiterate, and politically less conscious due to lack of information and political awareness, makes their choices based on suggestions from the male members of their families. As a result, women are left on the periphery of the political process.

In fact, even today, most of the women are uneducated; have little or no property and live in tradition bound societies. Women, especially in rural areas, would not come forward to stand and contest in the elections.

However, with the institution of Panchayati Raj women gained better participation in politics as well as in the decision making process.

Gender ideology plays a vital role in politics. Men and Women are differentiated psychologically, physiologically and also on intellectually. Women's perspective of life is looked down like and associated with the horizontal movements of waves and men's perception is looked up as if a ladder. Usually, women feel stressed more on attachments, affiliations, empathy and inter-dependence, but men mostly emphasize on competition, independence, separation and formal rights.

Gender empowerment requires changes in the systems, structures, attitudes and values. The real empowerment of women requires a thorough ongoing renewal of the political processes on a democratic basis so that they can be equipped with the necessary skills in political decision making and also their increased representation in the local bodies may not alter the existing setup. It is also necessary to sensitize the status of women from a women's perspective, not in the narrow feminist sense but in the sense of honourable co-existence with men, as this will enable women exercise their will and encourage them to have a complete emancipation.

To enhance self-potency and political efficacy, Women Organisations must have the support of politics and also they should maintain the political consciousness. This kind of extension brings greater affirmative action from the Panchayat to State and to National levels. If these measures are followed, women participation in politics will open up new vistas of development, which will automatically result in the real political empowerment of women in society (Krishna, B 2006).

Many respondents have highlighted the difficulties in active political participation. The factors that inhibit the participation in general are the backwardness of people, unwillingness to participate, absence of committed efforts, political interference, difficulty in availing funds, rigidity in programmes, etc. The obstacles to constructive participation include absence of organisations for the poor, limited access to technology, lack of local leadership, feudal agrarian structure, and hierarchical social relationships. Wolf, M (1983) says that class composition of the society and conflict among the under privileged group limit their political participation.

Attitude towards Political Activities

Empowerment enables individuals and groups to realize their full potential and capabilities that would enable them to be successful in all realms of life. Women empowerment would enable them to have better access to knowledge, skills and other resources. Participation of women in SHGs, NHGs and Gramasabhas is expected to bring about a desirable change in the attitude and perception of women towards political empowerment through participation. When asked about their attitude towards political participation, over one third (34.3%) of the respondents were of the opinion that participation in the SHGs/NHGs/Gramasabhas enabled them to acquire a positive attitude towards political participation to some extent and for another 8.7 per cent, the boost was to a great extent. This is a significant impact of participation in SHGs/NHGs/Gramasabhas even though for half of the respondents it did not make any impact. Political empowerment of SC women is further analysed with other independent variables and the findings is presented below.

Age and Attitude towards Political Activities

Women's political empowerment to a great extent depends on their organized movements. Grassroots level SHGs, NHGs and Gramasabhas provide a great opportunity for this. The experiences gained through the programmes of these grassroots level organisations would instill a positive attitude towards political participation. Age is an important variable that influence the attitudinal change of women towards political participation. It is expected that with age the chances of getting involved in women orgnisation and other social activities increases. The wider social exposure of elderly women would impart a positive and desirable change in their attitude towards political participation compared to the younger aged women. Attitudinal change of SC women belonging to different age groups is analysed and the findings in presented in the following table.

Table 6.1: Age and attitude towards political activities

Age	Attitude towards Political Activities					Total
	Increased to Great Extent (%)	Increased to some Extent (%)	Decreased to Great Extent (%)	Decreased to some Extent (%)	Remained the same (%)	
18-25	2 (4.1)	18 (36.7)	–	7 (14.3)	22 (44.9)	49
26-33	6 (6.5)	28 (30.1)	–	1 (1.1)	58 (62.4)	93
34-41	8 (9.8)	22 (26.8)	2 (2.4)	4 (4.9)	46 (56.1)	82
42 above	10 (13.2)	35 (46.1)	2 (2.6)	5 (6.6)	24 (31.6)	76
Total	26 (8.7)	103 (34.3)	4 (1.3)	17 (5.7)	150 (50)	300

** Significant at 1% level ($p<0.01$) $\chi^2 = 31.105$, df = 12, p-value 0.002

It is evident from the table that with increase in age, there is a positive change in the attitude of women towards political activities as a result of participation in women organizations. While 36.7 percentage of the respondents among the 18-25 age group experienced a positive attitudinal change to some extent and another 4.1 per cent experienced a significant level of attitudinal change in the positive directions; it is 46.1 per cent and 13.2 per cent respectively among the 42 years and above age category. This signifies the importance of age in bringing about a desirable change towards political participation of SC women. However the overall predominance of limited attitudinal change of SC women shows their overall backwardness and poor political consciousness. This is a very serious issue that needs immediate attention. Further, the issues of growing violence against SC women, character assassination and unscrupulous struggles for power pose serious challenges in the way of their political emancipation. The demanding nature of politics is another factor that limit the political participation of SC women. As is evident from the table, these issues can to a significant extent be solved through the participation of Dalit women in women organizations.

The significance of rural women folk can hardly be overlooked. The rural SC women are entrusted with the responsibilities of motherhood, household responsibilities and very often assist in earning a livelihood for the family which are not always visible and tangible in pure economic terms. This deprives them of political participation as manifested in the table. The χ^2 value calculated for 12 degrees of freedom is 31.105 with a corresponding p-value of 0.002. Hence we reject the null hypothesis and conclude that there is a significant relationship between age and attitudinal change of SC women who take part in government programmes towards political activities.

Education and Attitude towards Political Activities

Education is a key element in the political empowerment of SC women. Apart from widening the mental horizon of women, education enables to them to adhere to a rational and scientific approach towards life and society. It has direct implications on awareness, knowledge and perception of individuals. With higher levels of education, women are expected to develop a positive attitude towards political activities. Even though women in general have gained better political participation after the introduction of the Panchayati Raj system, looks bleak in terms of caste. When 20 per cent of women by the age of 25 to 45 years manage to gain some kind of political exposure (Devaki, 1996), 60 per cent of the elected representatives irrespective of sex difference still belong to the dominant castes. The following table presents the correlation between educational attainment and attitudinal change of SC women towards political participation.

The table 6.2 clearly indicates that education has a positive impact on the change of attitude among SC women. It is evident that when a significant proportion of graduate women (95.2%) manifest a positive inclination towards political activities, it is only 34.1 per cent in the case of Pre-degree holders and the proportion further declines to mere 24 per cent among the women with primary level of education. Higher proportion among the illiterate category simply means their blind following of leaders. Even though they participate in the political process, they are never part of decision making, the core of political activities. Education imparts the skills of identification of problem, analysis, decision making and problem solving. Direct participation coupled with these skills will definitely their political participation qualitative and meaningful.

Table 6.2: Education and attitude towards political activities

Education	Attitude towards Political Activities					Total
	Increased to Great Extent (%)	Increased to some Extent (%)	Decreased to Great Extent (%)	Decreased to some Extent (%)	Remained the same (%)	
Illiterate	7 (12.5)	25 (44.6)	2 (3.6)	4 (7.1)	18 (32.1)	56
Primary	8 (4.5)	43 (24)	2 (1.1)	10 (5.6)	116 (64.8)	179
Pre-degree	11 (25)	15 (34.1)	–	3 (6.8)	15 (34.1)	44
Graduate	–	20 (95.2)	–	–	1 (4.8)	21
Total	26 (8.7)	103 (34.3)	4 (1.3)	17 (5.7)	150 (50)	300

** Significant at 1% level ($p<0.01$) $\chi^2 = 76.702$, df = 12, p-value 0.005

When educated women participate voluntarily in the political process, they tend to openly express their scholarly views and opinions without fear. Education also facilitate women in easy communication with their colleagues and villagers with trust in a friendly manner. The χ^2 value calculated at 12 degrees of freedom is 76.702 for a corresponding p-value of 0.005. Hence by rejecting the null hypothesis a positive relationship between education and attitudinal change of SC women towards political activities it is established.

Occupation and Attitude towards Political Activities

Occupation of an individual is another important factor that shapes his perceptions, attitudes and values. The perception and attitude of a women who finds a job outside her home will be definitely different from a women who is engaged solely on household affairs. The role of institutionalized patterns like industries and educational institutions in shaping the values, attitudes and perceptions has been proved over time (Inkels, A 1976). It is manifested in the change of economic status and increased involvement in the socio-political activities. The following table presents the occupational category wise attitudinal change of SC women towards the political activities of SHGs, NHGs and Gramasabhas.

The table 6.3 shows that the highest proportion of positive change, either to some extent or to a great extent, in the attitude towards political activities through SHGs, NHGs and Gramasabhas took place among the employed category (63 per cent) followed by the self employed (43.5%) and unemployed (36.6%). For the labourers, the attitude towards political activities declined for the majority. This may be because of the fact that they due to illiteracy and preoccupation with their manual labour, they find little time to spare for SHGs, NHGs and Gramasabhas. A positive trend among the unemployed category is an indication that SHGs, NHGs and Gramasabhas are the only chances for these lots of women for social and political participation.

Table 6.3: Occupation and attitude towards political activities

Occupation	Attitude towards Political Activities					Total
	Increased to Great Extent (%)	Increased to some Extent (%)	Decreased to Great Extent (%)	Decreased to some Extent (%)	Remained the same (%)	
Employed	2 (3.7)	32 (59.3)	1 (1.9)	4 (7.4)	15 (27.8)	54
Self employed	3 (6.5)	17 (37)	1 (2.2)	1 (2.2)	24 (52.2)	46
labour	16 (12.9)	2 (1.6)	10 (8.1)	65 (52.4)	31 (25)	124
Unemployed	5 (6.6)	23 (30)	–	2 (2.6)	46 (60.5)	76
Total	26 (8.7)	103 (34.3)	4 (1.3)	17 (5.7)	150 (50)	300

** Significant at 1% level ($p<0.01$) $\chi^2 = 30.524$, df = 12, p-value 0.002

The χ^2 value calculated at 12 degrees of freedom is 30.524, for a corresponding p-value of 0.002. This proves the existence of a significant positive relationship between occupation SC women and their attitude towards political participation. Therefore, the null hypothesis is rejected.

Monthly Income and Attitude towards Political Activities

Independent income allows women a greater degree of freedom in household affairs and enables them to assert their standing in the decision making process. Such women are able to build self-esteem and negotiate in all important matters as they possess a dominant status with the family and society. The 73rd Amendment to the constitution opened up new avenues of social and political participation to these women. The grassroots level democratization and decentralization of power through the Panchayati Raj system enabled the erstwhile marginalized sections like the SC women to practice self governance. The relationship between the monthly income of the respondents and their attitudinal change towards political activities is presented in the following table.

The table 6.4 clearly depicts that with increase in monthly income the respondents develop a positive attitude towards the political participation through SHGs, NHGs and Gramasabhas. Their exposure and vast networks in their areas of work gives them confidence in managing public affairs and more over they are able to gain the support of their family members due to their dominant position in the family provided by their economic independence. When above three quarter of the respondents in the upper income group (Rs. 3001 and above) reckoned a positive change in their attitude towards political participation, the change is nominal (22.8%) for the lower income (Rs. 500 - 1000) category. In the case of the latter, their poor economic background, burden of household affairs, along with their educational backwardness deny them the opportunity to participate in the political arena offered by the local self governments.

Table 6.4: Monthly Income and attitude towards political activities

Monthly Income (Rs.)	Attitude towards political activities					Total
	Increased to Great Extent (%)	Increased to some (%) Extent	Decreased to Great Extent (%)	Decreased to some Extent (%)	Remained the same (%)	
501-1000	10 (6.3)	36 (22.8)	2 (1.3)	13 (8.2)	97 (61.4)	158
1001-3000	14 (13.2)	39 (36.8)	2 (1.9)	4 (3.8)	47 (44.3)	106
3001-above	2 (5.6)	28 (77.8)	–	–	6 (16.7)	36
Total	26 (8.7)	103 (34.3)	4 (1.3)	17 (5.7)	150 (50)	300

** Significant at 1% level ($p<0.01$) $\chi^2 = 48.084$, df = 8, p-value 0.005

The χ^2 value calculated at 8 degrees of freedom is 48.084, against a corresponding p-value of 0.005. Therefore by rejecting the null hypothesis we conclude that there exists a highly significant relationship between the monthly income of SC women and change in their attitude towards political activities of local democratic bodes.

Access to Political Leaders

Empowerment imparts knowledge, skills and competency to individuals which on the other hand instills the individuals with confidence, opens new avenues of opportunities and inter-personal relations. SC women empowered in such a way overcome all inhibitions and potentially more stronger. They also obtain the opportunities to meet other important personalities including the political leaders. For majority of the respondents, participation in the development programmes through PRIs provided them opportunities to meet political representatives for some reason or other. This factor is analyzed in the background of significant independent variables and the result is presented below.

Education and Access to Political Leaders

Education imparts moral strength and the most required confidence to appear in public. The morally elevated educated SC women who participate in the activities of SHGs/NHGs/Gramasabha often find the opportunity to meet political leader than the illiterates. The correspondence between the educational level of the respondents and their changes of meeting the political leaders is presented in the following table.

Table 6.5: Education and access to political leaders

Education	Access to Political Leaders				χ^2	df	p-value
	Very Often (%)	Often (%)	Never (%)	Total			
Illiterate	4 (7.1)	20 (35.7)	32 (57.1)	56	27.908**	6	0.005
Primary	22 (12.3)	110 (61.5)	47 (26.3)	179			
Pre-degree	8 (18.2)	26 (59.1)	10 (22.7)	44			
Graduate	5 (23.8)	14 (66.7)	2 (9.5)	21			
Total	39 (13)	170 (56.7)	91 (30)	300			

** Significant at 1% level ($p<0.01$)

It is evident that highly educated respondents meet political leaders more often than less educated ones. This trend is seen in both the categories who meet political leaders very often and often. When the 66.7 per cent of graduate respondents meet political leaders often and another 23.8 per cent meet them very often, for the illiterate category it is 35.7 per cent and 7.1 per cent respectively. This is a clear indication that when higher educated women participate in the activities of SHGs, NHGs, and Gramasabha, they are in a better position to utilize the opportunities offered by these institutional mechanisms.

The χ^2 value estimated for 6 degrees of freedom is 27.908 for a corresponding p-value of 0.005. Hence the null hypothesis can be rejected and can be oncluded that, the relationship between the SC women's educational level and their chances of meeting political leaders is highly significant.

Family Type and Access to Political Leaders

Type of family to a great extent determines the status of women. Traditional joint families are usually associated with the agrarian structure and religious orthodoxy. These families are dominated by conservative and rigid attitudes towards women. Hence traditionally women enjoyed less freedom in joint families compared to nuclear families. At the same time the women in joint families have the advantage of getting more time to meet the political leaders as the household responsibilities will be shared with other women in the house. It is also expected that women in nuclear families enjoy greater degree of freedom, flexibility and opportunities for self-expression. The relation between the family type of the respondents and their accessibility to the political leaders is presented in the following table.

Table 6.6: Family type and access to political leaders

Family Type	Access to Political Leaders				χ^2	df	p-value
	Very often (%)	Often (%)	Never (%)	Total			
Joint family	7 (4.5)	100 (63.7)	50 (31.8)	157	21.604**	2	0.005
Nuclear family	32 (22.4)	70 (49)	41 (28.7)	143			
Total	39 (3)	170 (56.7)	91 (30)	300			

** Significant at 1% level (p<0.01

The table clearly indicates that women hailing from nuclear families predominates among those who get chance to meet the political leaders very often (22.4 per cent). On the contrary, even though 63.7 per cent of SC women from joint families find chances to meet political leaders often, 31.8 per cent among them never get opportunities to meet their political leaders for any purpose.

The χ^2 value derived at for 2 degrees of freedom is 21.604 corresponding to a p-value of 0.005. Therefore, the null hypothesis is rejected and it can be concluded that the relationship between the respondents' family type and chances to meet their political leaders ishighly significant.

Monthly Income and Access to Political Leaders

Economic self-reliance is an important sign of empowerment of women. Economic freedom will bring with it social freedom that would enable women to move freely and meet their political leaders to enhance the activities of SHGs/NHGs/Gramasabha in which they are members. It is a common phenomenon that the economically well off sections have better social and political contacts. The monthly income of the respondents and their chances of meeting their elected representatives for different purposes is presented in the following table.

Table 6.7: Monthly Income and access to political leaders

Monthly Income (Rs.)	Access to Political Leaders				χ^2	df	p-value
	Very often (%)	Often (%)	Never (%)	Total			
501-1000	20 (12.7)	91 (57.6)	47 (29.7)	158	9.884**	4	0.042
1001-3000	16 (15.1)	51 (48.1)	39 (36.8)	106			
3001 above	3 (8.3)	28 (77.8)	5 (13.9)	36			
Total	39 (13)	170 (56.7)	91 (30.3)	300			

** Significant at 5% level (p<0.05)

It is evident from the table that with increase in monthly income, SC women get better chances of meeting their political leaders. Whereas 77.8

per cent of the respondents in the upper income category manage to meet their political leaders, it is only 57.6 per cent in the case of the lower income category (Rs. 501-1000). The lower proportion in the middle income category is an indication that they are mostly preoccupied with their day-to-day affairs to meet their both ends and, hence, find little time for social involvement. However, social involvement and political participation is an important weapon in the hands of SC women to break the chain of male chauvinism.

The χ^2 value derived at 4 degrees of freedom is 9.884 for a corresponding p-value of 0.042. Hence the null hypothesis can be rejected and can be concluded that there exists a highly significant relationship between SC women's monthly income and their chances of meeting their political leaders.

Participation in Political Campaigns

Women empowerment is a multi-dimensional and dynamic concept that covers social, political and economic aspects. Empowerment in these areas would enable women to acquire a dynamic personality which ultimately effect changes in their political perceptions. Participation in political campaigns is a means through which SC women get politically strengthened. Political campaigns ensure the strengthening of the participatory process by probing the vital energies of women and giving vent to their creative energies. Political participation of women also aims at raising their political awareness levels through constant conscientisation. Conscientisation would make women self organized and motivate them to undertake new initiatives (Santhosh, N 2003). Participation of SC women in political campaigns is assessed against significant independent variables and the result is discussed below.

Education and Participation in Political Campaigns

Political emancipation of the weaker sections through political campaigns is an important aim of PRIs. Participation in political campaigns is viewed as a means of socio-economic development of SC women. But this not an easy task as there are many constraints to achieve this end. However education is a strong instrument in achieving this end. The current declining tendency in participation in Gramasabhas indicates the need of real commitment on the part of citizens, local politicians and officials to organize campaigns for vitalizing this democratic and decentralized process (Patrick, H. Harilal, K.N and Chaudhuri, S 2007).

The table 6.8 given above clearly indicates that with improvement in educational standards of SC women their participation in the political campaign also increases. While majority of the graduate respondents (61.9%) informed that they very often participated in the political campaigns, it was only 12.5 per cent among the illiterate respondents. A notable feature is the participation level of women with primary education. In fact this may be claimed as the success of the NHGs/SHGs/ Gramasabh as to bring illiterate and primary educated women, otherwise would have remained within the four walls of their house, into limelight. However the overall poor educational level of SC women still makes the little efforts towards political emancipation of SC women futile.

Table 6.8: Education and participation in political campaigns

Education	Participation in Political Campaigns				χ^2	df	p-value
	Very Often (%)	Often (%)	Never (%)	Total			
Illiterate	7 (12.5)	25 (44.6)	24 (42.9)	56	42.954**	6	0.005
Primary	22 (12.3)	98 (54.7)	59 (33)	179			
Pre-degree	14 (31.8)	16 (36.4)	14 (31.8)	44			
Graduate	13 (61.9)	1 (4.8)	7 (33.3)	21			
Total	56 (18.7)	140 (46.7)	104 (34.7)	300			

** Significant at 1% level ($p<0.01$)

The value of χ^2 derived at for 6 degrees of freedom is 42.954 for a corresponding p-value of 0.005. In this circumstance the null hypothesis is rejected and it can be concluded that the relationship between educational attainment and participation in political campaign is highly significant.

Vandana Desai (2002) while writing on 'Informal Politics, Grassroots, NGOs and Women Empowerment in the Slums of Bombay' asserted the effectiveness of pernicious techniques of informal politics in effecting small but significant changes in their lives. She emphasized that success in personal power, power within, will subsequently lead to self empowerment and ultimately to involvement in political activism or power with and power to (Papart, *et.al.* 2002).

Family Type and Participation in Political Campaigns

SHGs usually involve in local political activities as it is important for getting assistance from various departments of the government. Local political activities here mean participation in the political campaigns of political parties, representation of the interests of SHGs before the political leadership or articulation of special political interests. SHGs, NHGs and Gramasabhas are open up opportunities to the grassroots level women to be part of such activities. Impact of family type of SC women on their involvement in the political campaigns is discussed here.

As per the table 6.9, there is no significant difference between respondents based on the type of their families with regard to their participation in political campaigns. Among the tradition bound, religious oriented, more closed and non-flexible joint family respondents 26.1 per cent confirmed that they always participated in the political campaigns;

whereas it is only 10.5 per cent among the respondents hailing from nuclear families. This seems to be good sign on the part of joint families as it reveals that joint families become more open in recent times.

Table 6.9: Family type and participation in political campaigns

Family Type	Participation in Political Campaigns				χ^2	df	p-value
	Always (%)	Some Times (%)	Never (%)	Total			
Joint family	41 (26.1)	60 (38.7)	56 (35.7)	157	14.923**	2	0.001
Nuclear family	15 (10.5)	80 (55.9)	48 (33.6)	143			
Total	56 (18.7)	140 (46.7)	104 (34.7)	300			

** Significant at 1% level ($p<0.01$)

However, the χ^2 value calculated for 2 degrees of freedom is 14.923 for a corresponding p-value of 0.001. This shows that the relationship between the respondents' family type is positively related to the participation of SC women in political campaigns. Hence the null hypothesis is rejected.

Occupation and Participation in Political Campaigns

As mentioned earlier, women's economic self-reliance is key to freedom in social and political affairs. Employment in the organized and unorganized sectors will make a difference in this regards. Usually, the employers in the organized sector will be more politically conscious as they will be members of some trade unions and bargaining forums; whereas those in the unorganized sector may not have this experience. The following table analyses this phenomenon among the respondents.

Table 6.10: Occupation and participation in political campaigns

Occupation	Participation in Political Campaigns				χ^2	df	p-value
	Always (%)	Some Times (%)	Never (%)	Total			
Employed	27 (50)	12 (22.2)	15 (27.8)	54	50.986**	6	0.005
Self employed	–	26 (56.5)	20 (43.5)	46			
Labour	15 (12.1)	67 (54)	42 (33.9)	124			
Unemployed	14 (18.4)	35 (46.1)	27 (35.5)	76			
Total	56 (18.7)	140 (46.7)	104 (34.7)	300			

** Significant at 1% level ($p<0.01$)

As expected it is evident from the table that employed section of the respondents predominate among those participate in the political campaigns. 50 per cent among them always participate in the political campaigns always. The labour category comes next, among whom 54 per cent participated in the political campaigns at least sometimes. The self-employed category seems to be the last as 43.5 per cent among them never participate in the political campaigns as they are mostly contained with their own activities. This reveals the advantage of being employed in the organized sector.

The χ^2 value for 6 degrees of freedom is 50.986 for a corresponding p-value of 0.005. Therefore the null hypothesis is rejected and it is concluded that the relationship between the occupation of SC women and their involvement in political campaigns is significant.

Monthly Income and Participation in Political Campaigns

The PRI is, in fact, a revolutionary mechanism in democracy that ensures people participation at grass root level for the implementation of developmental activities. But SC women's involvement in these activities to a large extent is influenced by their economic standing. The following table analyses the impact of monthly income of the respondents on the level of participation in political campaigns.

Table 6.11: Monthly income and participation in political campaigns

Monthly Income (Rs.)	Participation in Political Campaigns				χ^2	df	p-value
	Always (%)	Some Times (%)	Never (%)	Total			
501-1000	14 (8.9)	89 (56.3)	55 (34.8)	158	74.379**	4	0.005
1001-3000	17 (16)	46 (43.4)	43 (40)	106			
3001 above	25 (69.4)	5 (13.9)	6 (16.7)	36			
Total	56 (18.7)	140 (46.7)	104 (34.7)	300			

** Significant at 1% level ($p<0.01$)

It is evident that with increase in monthly income the intensity of participation of SC women in political campaign increases. When 69.4 per cent of the respondents in the upper income category always participate in the political campaigns it is 16 per cent and 8.9 per cent for the Rs. 1001-3000 and Rs. 501-1000 monthly income categories respectively. This may be considered as a significant indicator of the greater political and social freedom enjoyed by women with better personal incomes. The middle income category, again lags behind among the non-participants. This indicates the need of creating political consciousness among these sections of SC women.

The χ^2 value for 4 degrees of freedom is found to be 74.379, for a corresponding p-value of 0.005. This established a significant positive correspondence between SC women's monthly and their participation in political campaign. Hence the null hypothesis is rejected.

Lucy Lazo (1995) is of the opinion that says that involvement of women in small groups with the shared agenda will enable them to understand implicit processes of domination, organization and mobilization and put forward new inclusive political agenda that would lead to new forms of organization and action. Participation in SHGs, NHGs and Gramasabha is an important step forward in this line.

Opinion about Women Reservation Bill

Reservation had been ensured by the constitution of India to compensate the age old sufferings and oppression undergone by the weaker sections of society. Even though separate quotas have been reserved for SCs, STs, OBCs, minorities and physically challenged; no such reservation exists for women. Indian Parliament has witnessed heated discussions over the issue of women reservation and the bill for the same has been brought in the Parliament more than once but all in vain. This shows the political unwillingness of the political leaders. In this context that attitude of SC women towards women reservation has been sought in this study and the same has been analyzed on the background of different independent variables.

Age and Opinion about Women Reservation Bill

In the world's largest democracy like India, decentralization of power process will not be complete unless the full participation its women folk is ensured. Mere participation in the democratic process is not the sufficient condition for the political emancipation of SC women, rather their developmental goals needs to be realized. Without reservation political emancipation of these downtrodden lot will remain an oasis. Awareness of women about this situation is the primary step in attaining the goal. The following table represents the age wise opinion of the respondents about women reservation in the state legislatures and parliament.

Table 6.12: Age and Opinion about Women Reservation Bill

Age	Women Reservation Bill				χ^2	df	p-value
	Very Good (%)	Not useful for Women (%)	No idea (%)	Total			
18-25	30 (61.2)	1 (2)	18 (36.7)	49	37.159**	6	0.005
26-33	51 (54.8)	6 (5.5)	36 (38.7)	93			
34-41	51 (62.2)	4 (4.9)	27 (32.9)	82			
42 above	21 (27.6)	19 (25)	36 (47.4)	76			
Total	153 (51)	30 (10)	117 (39)	300			

** Significant at 1% level ($p<0.01$)

It is evident that the middle aged women (34-41) are more aware of the women reservation bill and are optimistic about it. The tradition bound elderly women (42years and above) do not feel very positive about the bill. The youngsters are also on the track as 61.2 per cent of them are positive about women reservation. The striking point is that almost half of the respondents in all age groups together are either not aware of the bill or do not feel positive about it. This figure points to the need of constant conscientisation of women on the issue of their reservation.

The χ^2 value for 6 degrees of freedom, for a corresponding p-value of 0.005, was found to be 37.159. Therefore the null hypothesis may be rejected and can be concluded that the relationship between the age of the respondents and their opinion about the reservation bill was significant.

Education and Opinion about Women Reservation Bill

Education important means through which women get awareness about the world around them. It makes them well informed, courageous and make informed decisions. The role of educated women in nation building is not in any way below that of men. The opinion of respondents regarding the women reservation bill on based on their educational level is given below.

Table 6.13: Education and opinion about women reservation bill

Education	Women Reservation Bill				χ^2	df	p-value
	Very Good (%)	Not useful for Women (%)	No idea (%)	Total			
Illiterate	7 (12.5)	13 (23.2)	36 (64.3)	56	67.641**	6	0.005
Primary	91 (50.8)	16 (8.9)	72 (40.2)	179			
Pre-degree	35 (79.5)	0.0	9 (20.5)	44			
Graduate	20 (95.2)	1 (4.8)	0.0	21			
Total	153 (51)	30 (10)	117 (39)	300			

** Significant at 1% level ($p<0.01$)

The table clearly shows the role of education in evaluating and arriving at an informed opinion about an issue. It is evident that as the level of education goes up SC women become more informed abut the role that reservation can play in their emancipation and hence feel positive about it. Thus, when 95.2 per cent of the graduate respondents have highly positive opinion about women reservation, it goes on decreasing as the education level of the respondents goes down which is manifested in the response of illiterate respondents. 64.3 per cent of them are not even aware of the bill and, hence, unable to take a stand. It is a fact that majority of the SC women get married at a very younger age which closes their chances of higher education and the only few lucky enough may get the opportunities for college education, which changes their opinion, belief and attitudes.

The χ^2 value calculated for 6 degrees of freedom (67.641) for a corresponding p-value of 0.005 also justifies the above analysis. Hence we can safely reject the null hypothesis and conclude that the relationship between the education of SC women and their opinion about the reservation bill are directly correlated.

Occupation and Opinion about Women Reservation Bill

It is vital for women to be engaged in some income generation activities as it will definitely improve their status within the family and outside. The SHGs and NHGs provide orientation to its members in this direction. The social orientation of individuals may vary according to the nature of the sector in which they are employed. Unlike the unorganized sector, the organized sector provides its employees wide platforms for getting exposure to social issues. Hence it is more likely that those employed in the organized sector will take informed decisions regarding public issues. Unfortunately, most of the SC women who have managed to find some occupation are employed in the unorganized sector which directly influences their perceptions and opinions. The following table represents the opinion of the respondents on the issue of women reservation bill based on the occupational status.

Table 6.14: Occupation and women reservation bill

Occupation	Women Reservation Bill				χ^2	df	p-value
	Very Good (%)	Not Useful for Women (%)	No idea (%)	Total			
Employed	42 (77.8)	2 (3.7)	10 (18.5)	54	39.696**	6	0.005
Self employed	24 (52.2)	9 (19.6)	13 (28.3)	46			
Labour	53 (42.7)	5 (4)	66 (53.2)	124			
Unemployed	34 (44.7)	28 (36.8)	14 (18.4)	76			
Total	153 (51)	30 (10)	117 (39)	300			

** Significant at 1% level (p<0.01)

It is seen that, the employed category of respondents are highly positive about the women reservation bill compared to other sections. When 77.8 per cent of the respondents commented positively about the women reservation bill, it is only 44.7 per cent among the unemployed category. It can also be noted that the laburers are the least informed category about the women reservation bill and the positive impacts it may have on them as most of them are illiterates and preoccupied with hard labor to make their both ends meet.

The χ^2 value calculated for 6 degrees of freedom (39.696) at a corresponding p-value of 0.005 also justifies the above said analysis that established a significant association between the occupational level and their opinion regarding women reservation bill. Therefore the null hypothesis can safely be rejected.

Monthly Income and Opinion about Women Reservation Bill

The type of freedom enjoyed by SC women with a regular satisfactory income is far beyond the reach of the unemployed and less income earners.

Status earned through regular income gives women the much required confidence and courage to move out of home and have their voice heard in public issues. The wider networks and contracts of these women strengthens them with information, and skills that enables them to take informed choices in personal and public issues.

Table 6.15: Monthly income and women reservation bill

Monthly Income (Rs.)	Women Reservation Bill				χ^2	df	p-value
	Very Good (%)	Not useful for Women (%)	No idea (%)	Total			
501-1000	74 (46.8)	19 (12)	65 (41.2)	158	12.990*	4	0.005
1001-3000	51 (48.1)	11 (10.4)	44 (41.5)	106			
3001 above	28 (77.8)	–	8 (22.2)	36			
Total	153 (51)	30 (10)	117 (39)	300			

** Significant at 5% level ($p<0.05$)

The table clearly points out that the perception of SC women on women reservation bill varies according to their monthly income. When over three forth (77.8%) of the upper income category (Rs. 3001 and above) appreciate the women reservation bill, the proportion of respondents who hold the same opinion among the lower income category (Rs. 501-1000) is only 46.8 per cent. Another trend that can be seen in the table is that awareness of SC women about the reservation bill and their capacity to take an informed decision about the bill increases with their increase in income. This is evident in the proportion of respondents who do not have any idea about the reservation bill which is merely 22.2 per cent among the upper income category where as it is 41.2 per cent among the lower income group.

The χ^2 value for 4 degrees of freedom for a corresponding p-value of 0.005 is calculated as 12.990. Therefore, by rejecting the null hypothesis we conclude that the relationship between the monthly income of the respondents and their opinion about the reservation bill is positively significant.

Conclusion

Political empowerment is the most significant element in the emancipation of the weaker sections of society. Actual development can be achieved without people's participation in the decision making process. This is really the true spirit of the participatory, decentralized democratic process. It is in this sense that Linz and Stepan, 1996 point out that discussion on democracy has shifted it focus from the study of transition to formal democratic rule to that of deepening democracy. The PRI offers a strong platform for the effective participation of SC women in the decision making process and thus deepening the the grassroots level democratic process.

In this chapter political empowerment of SC women and their attitude towards political activities have been discussed. It was found that participation in SHGs, NHGs and Gramasabhas helped 34.3 per cent of the respondents to improve their attitude towards political activities in a favourable direction. A cross variable analysis further proved that age, educational attainment, occupation and monthly income of SC women tended to show a significant positive association with their attitude towards political activities. The elderly, educated, employed and higher income categories of respondents have developed a favourable attitude towards political activities.

Having accessibility to the political leaders is another symptom of political empowerment. Involvement in the self-help groups provides opportunities to do so. But it was found that all sections of SC women were unable to utilize these opportunities. It was found that 56.7 per cent of the respondents could use the openings offered by the PRI and meet their political leaders for various purposes often. But another 30 per cent of the respondents failed to utilize this opportunity. Cross table analysis of the data further revealed that the predominant among those who could make use of the opportunities to meet the political leaders were the graduates and those hailing from nuclear families.

Participation in political campaigns was another area of political empowerment that was looked into. It was seen that when 46.7 per cent of the respondents often participated in the political campaigns 34.7 per cent kept aloof from it. Statistical calculations further revealed that the independent variables such as education, family type, occupation and income of SC women have statistically significant association with their attitude towards participating in political campaigns.

The political consciousness of SC women was assessed with their awareness and opinion about the women reservation bill. Surprisingly, 39 per cent of the respondents were not even aware of this bill. Considering the fact all the respondents were members of some SHGs/NHGs that provide opportunities for their socio-political empowerment, this finding points our fingers to the felt need of constant conscientisation of these downtrodden sections of society. Further analysis revealed that age at marriage, educational attainment, occupational category and income are important determinants in deriving at a positive attitude towards women reservation bill and ultimately political consciousness.

In shout, it can be said that the political empowerment of SC women are on the cross-roads. Even though SHGs, NHGs and Gramasabhas provide opportunities for their socio-political emancipation, they are unable to utilize them due to their low educational backwardness, low income and early marriages. Unless these issues are sorted, the political empowerment of SC women will remain an oasis in the desert.

7

Constraints in the Empowerment of Scheduled Caste Women

Women play a crucial role in the socio-economic development of any nation. Development of the nation will be incomplete and lopsided, until and unless women are fully involved in the process. In this sense, their emancipation is an essential pre-requisite in the way of economic and social upliftment of the nation. The effectiveness of development programmes depends on how vocal women are, how effective are they in taking decisions to their favour in male-dominated Panchayats so that there are some reductions in the arduous task faced by poor women. Unfortunately, women development programmes in the country are being challenged with traditional and cultural norms, lack of marketing and storage facilities, financial constraints, inadequate supply of inputs and lack of viability. This chapter is designed with the objective of analyzing these constraints. It recognizes the important linkages between family and acquisition of female literacy in developing countries, particularly in rural areas, and by addresses some of the important familial, socio-cultural, individual, and institutional factors that constrain women's empowerment. While the focus is Kerala, findings do have a wider application. Specifically, the findings of the study are presented to elicit feedback and insights, from the perspective of SC women, regarding the form, content, and operation of the PRI programs.

Resistance from Conservative Family Members

Despite their contributions to their households in terms of cash, as Lee (1997) points out, many women stay out of cooperatives due to the disturbances that it often causes among family members (Eber, 1993). Many people, especially elderly male members of the community, often criticize women who travel outside their communities to attend meetings and speak out in community assemblies. Women who do so are often subjected to brunt of rumors and gossips.

Women's stable income, apart from enabling them to gain economic independence, often makes their spouses depend on them. While women continue to uphold their core identities through weaving and food preparation, men can no longer rely on any specific occupation as a central aspect of their identities. Faced with the imbalance in traditional ideas about gender complementarity in work, women sometimes bring their spouse into cooperative work as advisors, mediators with outlets, or as "body guards" to protect them while carrying receipts. In general, spouses are supportive to the income generating activities of wives, but at one time or another most of them have shown resentment over their spouses' greater potentials.

Acquisition of literacy skills is a tedious task and added burden for women as they are endowed more with the survival related tasks of the family. There are 'time-bound' literacy plans and projects and poor women are easily blamed for their non-participation in such programmes due to poor motivation. Women have internalized a poor self-image and low self-esteem. Many of them have even regarded their inability to learn as natural and normal. Socialization reinforces the belief that, literacy is less significant for women due to the over expectations from their roles as wives and mothers.

Indian women are triply oppressed on the grounds of caste, gender and class. Grinding poverty and casteism erode health and well-being, and often make women doubt their personal worth. Nevertheless, at different points in their lives, most of them are oppressed by their own and others physical and psychological sufferings. In such situations, while, many men find a safety valve in alcohol and violent outbursts directed at their kin women, women usually internalize oppression in the forms of fear and low self-esteem. This very often prevents women from being involved in activities and organizations aimed at improving their lives.

Most women lack many of the technical skills required to compete in the global market. These skills range from the basic ones such as literacy and the use of postal service to the more advanced ones such as learning to create business plans and use computers.

Women's non-accessibility to markets and fair trade is a formidable obstacle in the way of realizing the transformative potential of cooperatives. Women friendly infrastructural facilities at different levels are required in the com-munities (e.g., roads, electricity, telephones and other forms of telecom-munications including fax machines and internet hookups). Women have to extend their contacts with exterior communities to establish commodity outlets. To facilitate this process, steps need to be taken to overcome the language barriers between indigenous communities and outside (including international) markets. Moreover, it is desirable to get rid of the monopolization of markets by middle men and merchants - both indigenous and non-indigenous.

It is needless to point out that, women empowerment is a pre-requisite for gaining collective strength which is necessary for building solidarity and support in the struggle against existing forces of oppression. If women have to fight against gender bias, they require strength acquired through the process of empowerment. Strengthening of capabilities of women is crucial for the liberation of the oppressed. But it is difficult to achieve this goal without removing the structural constraints that operate at various levels including the socio-economic, structural, ideological and political levels (Kaushik, 1993).

There are multitudes of interrelated reasons for the persistently high rate of unemployment among people with intellectual disability (Mank, 1994; Wehman and Kregel, 1995; Gosling and Cotterill, 2000; West et al., 1999). These include a lack of funding on ongoing support services and poorly defined procedures for the inclusion of people with severe disabilities.

Caste Identity

Caste is very often used a tool of domination and suppression in India. One can, therefore, easily presume that participation in local decision making is correlated with caste identities and the SCs are constrained to a great extent in voicing their opinions. SC women with their marginalized roles in the public sphere face many problems such as their wishes and thoughts often being neglected at the meetings, excluding them from improving their living standards and if at all women articulate their wants, they will not be credited for the achievements and might mostly be judged as ineffective and incapable. Furthermore the rural economy is often bartered with the male dominated agricultural produce where it is very difficult to estimate the *de facto* earnings and the people with almost no income are doomed to be ineligible for anything in their village. In the caste dominant Kerala society, Dalits are economically discriminated. They are significantly worse off compared to both the average of all other groups in Kerala or the SC population in India generally (Omvedt, 1998). Among the 300 respondents, 66 respondents' (22%) participation is hindered because of caste identity. For 48.3% of the respondents, participation is hindered sometimes and only for 29.7% of the respondents, participation is not hindered on account of their caste identities. The caste identity of SC women is correlated with other variables in following sections.

Age and Caste Identity

Women are confronted with the constraints that limit their potential for empowerment. These constraints operate at the individual, familial and societal levels and range from women's level of proficiency, knowledge, information, self-confidence etc, and the roles and relationships within the household to the societal constraints in terms of norms of behaviour for women (Johnson, 1999).

Table 7.1: Age and caste identities, hindered participation in the programmes

Age	Hindrance in Participation				χ^2	df	p-value
	Always (%)	Some times (%)	Never (%)	Total			
18-25	16 (32.7)	20 (40.8)	13 (26.5)	49	37.500**	6	0.005
26-33	11 (11.8)	41 (44.1)	41(44.1)	93			
34-41	9 (11)	50 (61.)	23 (28)	82			
42 above	30 (39.5)	34 (44.7)	12 (15.8)	76			
Total	66 (22)	145 (48.3)	89 (29.7)	300			

** Significant at 1% level ($p < 0.01$)

Table 7.1 highlights the age of the respondents and the hindrance that they face on account of their caste identity. Women in the age group of 42 years and above said that they were discriminated by the higher caste people. Even if they actively participated in the Gramasabha, SHGs, NHGs etc, they were ignored and disrespected in public. The upper caste people never mind to hear them, in any way, except at times. They never gave them any opportunity to do anything even if they were able to perform it well. Because of such discrimination, they themselves keep away from participating successfully in any programmes. The age groups between 18-25 years and 42 years and above were discriminated to some extent.

It is to be noted that about 26.5 per cent the informants from age group of 18-25 years and 44.1 per cent of SC women in the age group of 26-33 years felt that they never faced any type of discrimination. Similarly, the respondents belonging to the 34-41 age group have not faced such type of discrimination faced by the women in the age group of 42 years and above. It may be because the youngsters maintain friendly relation with every one, or the higher caste people feel shame to show such type of discrimination in common platforms or the youngsters are well aware of the court and orders.

The χ^2 calculated for 6 degrees of freedom is 37.500 and its p-value is 0.005. This confirms that the correlation between age and caste identities with hindered participation in the programmes is more significant.

Education and Caste Identity

Recognizing the importance of education as the most powerful instrument for empowering the socially disadvantaged groups, the Ninth Plan envisaged universalization of primary education by 2005 with a special focus on low-literacy pockets and on the educationally backward communities like SCs, OBCs and the Minorities. Illiteracy makes individuals unreflective and hinders them from giving thoughtful judgements on issues of importance. Education facilitates the development of a progressive attitude towards social and economic problems (Bhat, K.S 1967). An attempt is made to analyse the relationship between education and SC women's propensity to participate in SHGs/NHGs and the result is given in the following table.

Table 7.2: Education and caste identities, hindered participation in the programmes

Education	Hindrance in Participation				χ^2	df	p-value
	Always (%)	Some times (%)	Never (%)	Total			
Illiterate	23 (41.1)	19 (33.9)	14 (25)	56	46.350**	6	0.005
Primary	20 (11.2)	98 (54.7)	61 (34.1)	179			
Pre-degree	10 (22.7)	20 (45.5)	14 (31.8)	44			
Graduate	13 (61.9)	8 (38.1)	–	21			
Total	66 (22)	145 (48.3)	89 (29.7)	300			

** Significant at 1% level ($p<0.01$)

Table 7.2, indicates the educational status of the sample population with respect to caste identities. It is to be noted that, most of the graduates (61.9%), 22.7% of the Pre-degree holders and 41.1% of the illiterate respondents felt that that they were always being hindered from participating in the programme aimed at their social emancipation. Both the illiterates and the educated alike among the SC women were neglected by the upper caste people. Such discrimination, unlike in other communities, prevents SC women from demonstrating their abilities despite of their educational qualifications.

Illiteracy, ignorance, lack of motivation, lack of experience and lack of communication are key factors behind the social taboo faced by the SC women. Bhattacharya (2002) points out that the lack of experience is another obstacle that the women face. They require adequate continuous guidance and time to time training to overcome this difficulty. They are not trained by the people (male) to take initiatives and to sustain their activities. They face difficulties and mental distress.

The SC Graduate women were of the opinion that the elite groups never tried to acknowledge their strength, promote their aspiration levels, mobilize and channelize their resources for productive purposes. They did not have good influence and were generally ignored. The poor SC women shrink inside the barriers as their higher authorities show superiority over them and their work. The elite groups dehumanize their moral worth. They are neither glorified and supported nor allowed to shine in their work places.

The upper caste people in no way inspire the poor Dalit women to come up in their life. Instead they are being suppressed to the bottom. They face problems in all the fields they work. These are the reasons why they are not participating in NHGs, SHGs and Gramasabha. The discrimination, humiliation and neglect that the SC women experience are purely because of their caste identity.

The χ^2 value calculated for 6 degrees of freedom is 46.350 with a p-value of 0.005. Therefore the null hypothesis can be ignored and can be concluded that irrespective of their educational qualifications, the caste identity of SC women hinder their participation in the programmes.

Family Type and Caste Identity

A peasant woman's life in rural India is characterized with backbreaking work with little personal freedom and strict adherence to rigid social norms. Extended family is the major feature of this farming economy. Most of the families in an agrarian village are joint families dominated by the elderly. Every aspect of the young couple's interaction, seemingly, is controlled by the family elders in the family. There is little space or opportunity for the building a close relationship based on companionship. For woman, sexual act is just the necessary obligation of married life, the principal aim of which is to furnish male children to the family. Women are aware of and are do hate the complete regulation of their personal lives but feel themselves powerless to change their circumstances. Any attempt to loosen the bonds imposed on these women must be sensitive and responsive to these realities of their daily life and to their perceptions of the situation (Dandekar, H 1981). A detailed analysis is presented in the table below in which the family type of the respondents is related with their caste identity which hinders their participation in SHGs, NSGs or Gramasabha.

Table 7.3: Family type and caste identities that hinder participation in the programmes

Family Type	Hindrance in Participation				χ^2	df	p-value
	Always (%)	Some times (%)	Never (%)	Total			
Joint family	46 (29.3)	76 (48.4)	35 (22.3)	157	14.014**	2	0.001
Nuclear family	20 (14)	69 (48.3)	54 (37.8)	143			
Total	66 (22)	145 (48.3)	89 (29.7)	300			

** Significant at 1% level ($p<0.01$)

Table 7.3 shows that women in joint families (29.3%) are more suppressed from participating in these programmes than those hail from nuclear families (14%). In the joint family, women play an all-round role as a spider in the web. She has to take care of all the needs in the house. As their families are basically poor, they are forced to support the family by working and as a result, they are not able to spare time to spend in the governments supportive structures (SHGs, NHGs, Gramasabha). She should take care of her in-laws and husband. Their in-laws scold them if they are active outside the household since this could create a bad reputation for the family. Controls on mobility are often imposed by women themselves on their own daughters, sisters, daughters-in-law and other female relatives.

If SC women are unable to attend the meetings in these groups, the elites insult, ill-treat and degrade them. The SC women often limit their participation in local the decision-making processes and often keep out of the SHGs, NHGs and Gramasabha.

The χ^2 calculated for 2 degrees of freedom is 14.014 and its p-value is 0.001 and by pass the null hypothesis. It can be concluded that the family type of the sample respondents is strongly associated with their caste identities and hinder their participation in the programmes.

Occupation and Caste identity

Employment, particularly for cash and in non- traditional occupations, potentially empowers women by providing financial independence and alternative sources of social identity. An attempt is made to bring out the relationship between the caste identity of SC women which hinders the participation with their occupation.

Table 7.4: Occupation and caste identities that hinder participation in the programmes

Occupation	Hindrance in Participation				χ^2	df	p-value
	Always (%)	Some times (%)	Never (%)	Total			
Employed	28 (51.9)	18 (33.3)	8 (14.8)	54	38.738**	6	0.005
Self employed	10 (21.7)	26 (56.5)	10 (21.7)	46			
Labour	18 (14.5)	64 (51.6)	42 (33.9)	124			
Unemployed	10 (13.2)	37 (48.7)	29 (38.2)	76			
Total	66 (22)	145 (48.3)	89 (29.7)	300			

** Significant at 1% level ($p < 0.01$)

From table 7.4, it can be seen that the unemployed SC women (38.2%) never faced any problems in participating in SHGs because they have attended the meeting regularly, go neatly, grasp everything clearly, do their duty in time. On the other hand, the employed SC women (51.9%) faced problems because of rivalry among themselves and from the elite people in their offices. The high ranking castes, often, show discriminate and insult them. Despite the SC women's struggle for existence in the groups, they are not recognised by the other people. They face many problems in the NHGs and SHGs, and are not able to concentrate and work with good spirit. So they are not participating actively in such programmes.

The χ^2 calculated for 6 degrees of freedom is 38.738 and its p-value is 0.005. By ignoring the null value, it is concluded that the occupation of the SC women is strongly related with the caste identities and hinder their participation in the programmes.

Monthly Income and Caste Identity

The monthly income of the respondents is correlated with their caste identity, which hinder their participation in the programs meant for them and the result is presented in the following table.

Table 7.5: Monthly income and caste identities that hinder participation in the programmes

Monthly Income (Rs.)	Hindrance in Participation				χ^2	df	p-value
	Always (%)	Some times (%)	Never (%)	Total			
501-1000	21 (13.3)	79 (50)	58 (36.7)	158	59.557**	4	0.005
1001-3000	20 (18.9)	61 (57.5)	25 (23.6)	106			
3001-above	25 (69.4)	5 (13.9)	6 (16.7)	36			
Total	66 (22)	145 (48.3)	89 (29.7)	300			

** Significant at 1% level ($p < 0.01$)

Table 7.5, reveals how the SC women are hindered in participating in SHGs, NHGs and Gramasabha. 13.3 per cent among the monthly income earners of Rs.501-1000 always faced several problems in the name of caste and creed. 50 per cent of the respondents reported that they did not face it often, and 36.7 per cent of the sample respondents of the same category reported that they never faced it at all.

Among the monthly income earners in the range of Rs. 1001-3000, 18.9 percent of the respondents often faced the same problem. 57.5 per cent of the respondents faced it sometimes, and 23.6 per cent of the respondent said that they have never faced it at all. 69.50 per cent of the income earners in the range of Rs. 3001 and above always faced the constraints of caste identity and 13.9 per cent said that they faced it sometimes and 16.7 per cent stated that they never faced it at all.

It is obvious that the sample respondents have faced humiliations on the basis of caste, creed or colour, which is not tolerable to the SC women, in all the platforms they go. They were suppressed by the upper castes and the male dominated society. How will they be empowered if they are being continued to be suppressed even after all the constitutional amendments aimed at their empowerment? It is evident that the SC women who earn more income are prone to face more constraints than the low income earners.

The Chi-square calculated for 4 degrees of freedom is 59.557 with the p-value of 0.005 shows that the monthly income has significant relation with the caste identities and the way they were hindered in participating in the programs.

Free Time

Women are, indeed, eager to attend Gramasabha meetings and to participate in the process of decision making. But, unfortunately the deeply extended caste and patriarchy structures impose greater restrictions on the involvement of women in these institutional structures. Rural women might show reluctance to participate these systems for many reasons. They are often busy in their household activities and farm work and are unable to find enough spare time for participation. Some of them feel inhibited to participate for reasons such as lack of confidence, family pressures, customs, etc. (Mukherjee, N 1993). Among the 300 respondents, only 88 respondents (29.3%) find time always to participate in the programs, The majority (58%) fairly had time to spare and 38 (12.7%) did not find any time at all to participate in the programs.

Education and Free Time

Education is an eye opener in our life which is essentially social in character (Mukharji, A and Neelam,V 1987).

Table 7.6: Education and free time

Education	Free time				χ^2	df	p-value
	Always (%)	Some times (%)	Never (%)	Total			
Illiterate	14 (25)	37 (66.1)	5 (8.5)	56	25.042**	6	0.005
Primary	40 (22.3)	114 (63.7)	25 (14)	179			
Pre-degree	21 (47.7)	18 (40)	5 (11.4)	44			
Graduate	13 (61.9)	5 (23.8)	3 (14.3)	21			
Total	88 (29.3)	174 (58)	38 (12.7)	300			

** Significant at 1% level ($p < 0.01$)

Table 7.6 shows that graduate women (61.9%) found enough spare time to participate in these programmes, than the primary educated and illiterates groups. The graduates may work in different places, sometimes far away from home. It may take time for them to reach home on time, they may have to do over time duty in their offices and when they reach home they have to take care of their kins, in-laws and often bed-ridden parents. Only on Sundays they are busy with washing and ironing the clothes of the family members. Naturally, they do not get spare time to spare for other programmes.

The illiterate women (74.6%) are also not getting enough time because they are always busy with house hold works, away from their homes and face the above said problems. The respondents felt that they are not capable to participate because they are not much educated and they feel very shy. In spite of positive family environment, perhaps the educational backwardness might have served as a barrier to participation. Organizing the family, social as well as religious engagements on Sundays and other holidays will have a negative impact on the participation of women.

The χ^2 value calculated for 6 degrees of freedom is 25.042 and its p-value is 0.005. By ignoring the null value it can be stated that the education of the SC women is strongly related to the time to spare and hindrance in their participation in the programmes.

Occupation and Free Time

The economic obstacle is also important. Women in rural areas play a direct role in the income generating activities. Most of them work in the unorganized sectors and support their male counterparts in earning their livelihood. In some families, they are the principal bread earners. Apart from this, they are accountable for the household work. Increasing poverty forces them to play both the roles of looking after the household work as well as the bread earning activities. In most cases it is decided by the attitude of the partners towards household affairs and their relative control over the economic resources. If both the partners view housework as an unpleasant necessity, the person with fewer resources will do more of it, because she/he has more to lose if the union dissolves (England and Farkas, 1986).

Table 7.7: Occupation and free time

Occupation	Free Time				χ^2	df	p-value
	Always (%)	Some times (%)	Never (%)	Total			
Employed	41 (75.5)	11 (20.4)	2 (3.7)	54	70.161**	6	0.005
Self employed	7 (15.2)	31 (67.4)	8 (17.4)	46			
Labour	24 (19.4)	84 (67.7)	16 (12.9)	124			
Unemployed	16 (21.1)	48 (63.2)	12 (15.8)	76			
Total	88 (29.3)	174 (58)	38 (12.7)	300			

** Significant at 1% level (p<0.01)

The table above presents the occupational status of the sample respondents and their participation. Employed women (75.5%) get enough spare time to participate in these programmes. As their office time is from 9.30 A.M to 5.00 P.M some get official vehicles, they reach home on time. The employed women know the values of SHGs, NHGs etc. So they find enough time to participate in these programmes.

Empowerment is a good platform to solve many of the problems they face that cannot be solved by legal measures. The developmental programmes are designed at the grass root level. The employed know about the government agencies that are seen as means of ensuring democratic participation of SC women. Most of the studies deal with women's domestic work and occupational outside home for women means they have to perform two independent roles resulting in role- conflicts (Myrdal and Klen 1956; Sethi 1978; Mies 1980; Mathur 1992).

The χ^2 value calculated for 6 degrees of freedom is 70.161 with a p-value of 0.005. Thus, by ignoring the null value it can be concluded that the occupation of SC women is strongly related with the time to spare and their participation in the programmes.

Monthly Income and Free Time

An attempt is made blow to analyse the monthly income of the respondents with the free time they find to spare for the developmental activities.

Table 7.8: Monthly Income and free time

Monthly Income (Rs.)	Free Time				χ^2	df	p-value
	Always (%)	Some times (%)	Never (%)	Total			
501-1000	38 (24.1)	106 (67.1)	14 (8.9)	158			
1001-3000	25 (23.6)	57 (53.8)	24 (22.6)	106	44.388**	6	0.005
3001-above	25 (69.4)	11 (30.6)	–	36			
Total	88 (29.3)	174 (58)	38 (12.7)	300			

** Significant at 1% level ($p < 0.01$)

Table 7.8 highlights that 69.4 per cent of the respondents who earn a monthly income above Rs.3000, find enough time to participate in the SHGs, NHGs and Gramasabha. Their major income generation activities are animal husbandry, poultry, soap and umbrella making which are a major thrust area of SHGs and NHGs. They generate their income regularly from the above sources which enables them to acquire a better status in the society and within the family.

The low income earners women, (below Rs.3000) face many problems within their families and in the society they live. They live in rented house, are burdened with more responsibilities, and are forced to work day and night. This deteriorates their health. The economic situation and social structure make the situation worse. So they are not able to participate in these programmes. Another notable point is that 22.6 per cent of the respondents, whose monthly income is in the range of Rs. 1001-3000, never participate in the as they are not being provided with prior information about the meetings by the officials.

The χ^2 calculated for 6 degrees of freedom is 44.388 with a p-value of 0.005. Hence by ignoring the null value, it can be state that, there is a significant relationship between the monthly income of the SC women, time to spare, and participation in the programmes.

Family Restrictions

The family's restrictions and the social pressure on women who join public activities are extraordinarily high. For those who are married, the pressure of public life is eased to some extent by their class situation. In many cases, the joint family system or at least a strong family never supports women to participate in outdoor programs. However, the constraints imposed by family continue to be a real concern even for privileged women. Among the 300 respondents, 23 (7.7%) always faced restrictions to go out to participate in the programs, 125 (41.7) were sometimes restricted, and 152 (50.7%) never had any restriction to go out of the home and participate in the programs.

Age and Family Restrictions

Age plays an effective role in the Indian families; it is presumed that the people in their tender age are not able to make decisions wisely. Added to it, women are in bounded restrictions for each and every thing, whatever they do.

Table 7.9: Age and family restriction to go outside home

Age	Restriction to go out of Home				χ^2	df	p-value
	Always (%)	Some times (%)	Never (%)	Total			
18-25	–	18 (36.7)	31 (63.3)	49	14.1543**	6	0.024
26-33	8 (8.6)	42 (45.2)	43 (46.2)	93			
34-41	7 (8.5)	26 (31.7)	49 (59.8)	82			
42 above	8 (10.5)	39 (51.3)	29 (38.2)	76			
Total	23 (7.7)	125 (41.7)	152 (50.7)	300			

** Significant at 1% level ($p < 0.01$)

Table 7.9 reveals that women in the age group of 42 years and above (51.3%) were restricted by their family members to go outside the home and participate in the programmes. It is only because they are aged, their health conditions, and over burden in their home. Their husbands and in-laws restrict them to go to the Gramasabha as both males and females participate in these. The males may harass women in public. But in the case of SHGs, the women are not restricted, as they are women only agencies. When women are forced to go to the market, they are denied the opportunity to participate in Gramasabha. This is, indeed, a pathetic situation.

But the tender aged women manage to attend such functions because the younger generation knows more about these programmes. The χ^2 calculated for 6 degrees of freedom is 14.1543 and its p-value is 0.024. Hence, by not taking into account the null value, it is concluded that the age of the sample respondents has a strong bearing on the restrictions imposed by their family members on the basis of caste identities in participating in the programmes.

Education and Family Restriction

Education acts as a major catalyst in improving the status of women. Education for rural women is more important, especially for the members of the political institutions as it will help them to understand the rules and regulations of the institution and fulfill the objectives of the PRI and carry out their day to day functions. Even though women have much to do in the society for the welfare of her surroundings, often her family restricts her in all her ways by denying her even proper education. The relation between education and family's restriction is presented in detail in the table below.

Table 7.10: Education and Family restriction to go outside home

Education	Restriction to go out of Home			Total	χ^2	df	p-value
	Always (%)	Some times (%)	Never (%)				
Illiterate	2 (3.6)	28 (50)	26 (46.4)	56	25.814**	6	0.005
Primary	20 (11.2)	79 (44.1)	80 (44.7)	179			
Pre-degree	1 (2.3)	17 (38.6)	26 (59.1)	44			
Graduate	–	1 (4.8)	20 (95.2)	21			
Total	23 (7.7)	125 (41.7)	152 (50.7)	300			

** Significant at 1% level ($p<0.01$)

Table 7.10 projects that, 95.2 per cent of the graduate respondents were never restricted by their family members to work outside. Education plays a major role in enabling them to participate in these programmes. The educated husband and in-laws know exactly of what is happening in the SHGs and Gramasabha meetings. The family members support them to attend the meetings even at late hours. But this is not the case with the illiterate SC women.

The freedom of movement is strongly related with empowerment through education. Majority of educated women move with complete freedom, which shows greater self-esteem, self-confidence, self-knowledge, etc. Half of the illiterate respondents never enjoyed freedom of movement to participate in these programmes.

The χ^2 calculated for 6 degrees of freedom at 25.814 with a p-value of 0.005 indicates that the null hypothesis can be ignored and it can be concluded that the educational level of the sample respondents is strongly related with the restriction to go out of home and participate in the programmes.

Family Type and Restriction

The family structure is generally distinguished as joint and nuclear. Joint family is associated with traditional and agricultural society where conservatism and family status tend to dominate over individual interests.

On the other hand, nuclear family is more prone to mobility, industrialized society and permits greater degree of flexibility and self expression among members. The traditional approach generally measures the socio-economic inequalities in terms of consumption, education, or income. In the absence of broad based pension or other social security schemes, traditional living arrangements, where the majority of the older adults are supported by their children or extended family, provided a form of social net (Rajan, Mishra, and Sharma, 1999). The survey results in this regard are presented in the table below.

Table 7.11: Family type and Family restriction to go outside home

Family Type	Restriction to go out of Home				χ^2	df	p-value
	Always (%)	Some times (%)	Never (%)	Total			
Joint family	16 (10.2)	52 (33.1)	89 (56.7)	157	10.867**	2	0.004
Nuclear family	7 (4.9)	73 (51)	63 (44.1)	143			
Total	23 (7.7)	125 (41.7)	152 (50.7)	300			

** Significant at 1% level ($p < 0.01$)

Table 7.11 highlights the family type and their restriction to go out of home which can be seen as a sign the autonomy of women. The results very clearly points outs that the nuclear family members often faced the restriction to go outside home because of the suspicious husbands and they have kids. But in the joint family, the presence of in-laws restricts the autonomy of women. The SC women living in joint families face an orthodox situation in their new homes and are restricted to go out with or without permission. Thus the women staying in nuclear families have the highest level of autonomy compared to those living in joint families. Women who have highest level of autonomy are more empowered empowerment.

The χ^2 value calculated for 2 degrees of freedom is 10.867 and its p-value of 0.004. Thus by ignoring the null value, it is concluded that the family type of the sample respondents is strongly related to the restriction to go out of home to participate in the programmes.

Occupation and Family Restrictions

Employment is an activity or service performed for somebody else especially for compensation or as an occupation (Merriam-Webster Dictionary of Law, 1996). The majority of the respondents enter the labor force due to economic compulsion and the benefits of their economic contributions were mediated to the families. But women are often restricted to go out of home to participate in the programs like SHGs. The survey result in this regard is presented in the table below.

Table 7.12: Occupation and family restriction to go outside home

Occupation	Restriction to go out of Home				χ^2	df	p-value
	Always (%)	Some times (%)	Never (%)	Total			
Employed	–	18 (33.3)	36 (66.7)	54	18.010**	6	0.006
Self employed	5 (10.9)	21 (45.7)	20 (45.5)	46			
Labour	6 (4.6)	57 (46)	61 (49.2)	124			
Unemployed	12 (15.8)	29 (38.2)	35 (46.1)	76			
Total	23 (7.7)	125 (41.7)	152 (50.7)	300			

** Significant at 1% level ($p < 0.01$)

The above table shows the extent to which occupation restricts SC women from going out of home to participate in SHGs and Gramasabha meetings. It is to be noted that the employed respondents are rarely restricted to go out to attend such meetings. But the self-employed respondents (45.7%) are constrained by their family members as they see attending these meetings as waste of time and loss of income. 46.1 percent of the unemployed, 49.2 per cent of labourers, felt that they were not restricted on the basis of occupation. Women are made to work like machines for the sake of her family, and their freedom is being restricted.

The χ^2 calculated for 6 degrees of freedom is 18.010 with a p-value of 0.006; hence by ignoring the null value, it can be stated that the occupation of the sample respondents has a significant relationship with the restriction to go out of home and participate in the programmes.

Monthly Income and Family Restrictions

In rural areas, it is hardly possible to expect people to talk about their incomes in actual figures. This difficulty is even more real when it comes to women who in most cases are not quiet conversant about family income, property or wealth and who find it hard to make monetary assessments. To such questions they turned to their husbands, brother-in-law or father-in-law for answer. The table below represents the relationship between monthly income and family's restriction to go out of home to participate in the programs.

Table 7.13 demonstrates that majority of respondents (55.1 %) earning very low income category (Rs.501-1000 per month) mentioned that they were hindered to go out of home and participate in SHGs and Gramasabha meetings because their family members restricted them by telling that there is no meaning in attending such meetings. It is clearly understood from the table that those who earn more than 3000 per month were not at all prevented from attending such meetings.

Table 7.13: Monthly income and family restrict to go outside home

Monthly Income (Rs.)	Restriction to go out of Home				χ^2	df	p-value
	Always (%)	Some times (%)	Never (%)	Total			
501-1000	12(7.6)	87(55.1)	59(37.3)	158	31.527**	4	0.006
1001-3000	11(10.4)	30(28.3)	65(61.3)	106			
3001-above	–	8(22.2)	28(77.8)	36			
Total	23(7.7)	125(41.1)	152(50.7)	300			

** Significant at 1% level ($p < 0.01$)

The χ^2 value calculated for 4 degrees of freedom is 31.527 and its p-value is 0.006, based on which we ignore the null value and conclude that the monthly income of the sample respondents is strongly related to the restriction to go out of home to participate in the programmes.

Compromise the Occupation Schedule

Women themselves may be incorporated into the social and economic life which limits their control over their lives and livelihoods. Thus, equally relevant issues for the analysis may be constrained and unfavorable or adverse incorporation (Bracking, 2003). Once women decide to work or are forced to work, what they can do is being shaped by norms regarding appropriate work for women and influencing women's terms of inclusion. Occupational segregation limits women to the least remunerated occupations or sectors of occupational groups (Salway et al., 2005). According to Salway, women try to make benefits by working hard to supplement their family with income. Women in the rural areas compromise their occupational schedule to work in the development programs. Among the 300 respondents, 31 (10.3%) were always asked to favour their occupation schedule to participate in the developmental programs, 190 respondents (63.3%) were asked to favour some times, and 79 (26.3%) were not asked to favour their occupational schedule.

Education and Occupation Schedule Compromise

Education is a medium to empower women by equipping them with the information and the means of functioning effectively. With respect to the respondents' education, they compromise their time from their occupation schedule. This problem is presented in the table below.

Table 7.14: Education and compromise the occupation schedule

Education	Compromise the Occupation Schedule				χ^2	df	p-value
	Always (%)	Some times (%)	Never (%)	Total			
Illiterate	3 (5.4)	45 (80.4)	8 (14.3)	56	65.410**	6	0.005
Primary	7 (3.9)	119 (66.5)	53 (29.6)	179			
Pre-degree	10 (22.7)	22 (50)	12 (12)	44			
Graduate	11 (52.4)	4 (19)	6 (28.6)	21			
Total	31 (10.3)	190 (63.3)	79 (26.3)	300			

** Significant at 1% level ($p < 0.01$)

From the table 7.14, it is understood that the graduate respondents (52.4%) compromised to change their occupation schedule for participating in the developmental activities, because the graduates have more capability to grasp, give new ideas, and give solution for problems. The learned women know more about these programmes, what do these programmes mean, what necessary steps should be taken to develop these programmes in their localities, and so on. They can promote people to join in these programmes by telling the facts about these programmes and how do they work. These programmes are organized with the aim of emancipation of grass roots and to empower the women.

The χ^2 calculated for 6 degrees of freedom is 65.410 and its p-value is 0.005. Hence by ignoring the null value, it is concluded that the sample respondents' compromise of their occupation schedule to participate in the programmes has a direct bearing on their monthly income.

Family Type and Compromise on the Occupation Schedule

The type of family in which women live is more important for her to spare her valuable time for some other purpose like attending the development programmes. Here in the table below the family type is correlated with the effort to compromise time for the development programs.

Table 7.15: Family type and the occupation schedule compromise

Family Type	Compromise the Occupation Schedule				χ^2	df	p-value
	Always (%)	Some times (%)	Never (%)	Total			
Joint family	25 (15.9)	92 (58.6)	40 (25.5)	157	11.128**	2	0.004
Nuclear family	6 (4.2)	98 (68.5)	39 (27.3)	143			
Total	31 (10.3)	190 (63.3)	79 (26.3)	300			

** Significant at 1% level ($p < 0.01$)

Table 7.15 displays the situations of women hailing from different families. 15.9% of the respondents from the joint families were allowed to compromise their occupational schedules to attend these programmes. Joint family is a large one, and in such families, many are working. If they spare their time for these programmes their family will not suffer. But in the case of women from nuclear families, they cannot spare their time, because they will be over involved in the family affairs. If the wife is a working she may not find time to spare as her family will suffer a lot for each and everything.

The χ^2 value calculated for 2 degrees of freedom is 11.128 with a p-value of 0.004, thus, by ignoring the null value, it is concluded that the family type of the sample respondents has a significant bearing on the possibility of compromising their occupation schedule to participate in the programmes.

Occupation and the Occupation Schedule Compromise

It is true that any employed person, whether salaried worker or self-employed, may have greater control over their lives than domestic workers. This is true in the case of SC women as well. Hence it is likely that most employed women concentrate in the development activities by compromising their occupational schedule.

Table 7.16: Occupation and compromise the occupation schedule

Occupation	Compromise the Occupation Schedule			Total	χ^2	df	p-value
	Always (%)	Some times (%)	Never (%)				
Employed	21 (38.9)	19 (35.2)	14 (25.9)	54			
Self employed	2 (4.3)	39 (84.8)	5 (10.9)	46			
Labour	6 (4.8)	91 (73.4)	27 (21.8)	124	78.912**	6	0.005
Unemployed	2 (2.6)	41 (53.9)	33 (43.4)	76			
Total	31 (10.3)	190 (63.3)	79 (26.3)	300			

** Significant at 1% level (p <0.01)

Table 7.16 displays the occupational level of the sample respondents in relation with compromising their occupational schedule. 38.9 per cent of the employed SC women always get chance to compromise their occupation schedule for participating in the developmental activities. The employed women earn sufficient income, at least they can spend enough money for a month, but women in the other three categories do not earn sufficient income and if they spare their time in these programmes their families will suffer badly.

The χ^2 calculated at 6 degrees of freedom is 78.912 and its p-value is 0.005. Therefore, by disposing the null value, it can be stated that the correlation between occupation and the chance of compromising the occupational schedule to participate in the programmes is more significant.

Monthly Income and Compromise the Occupation Schedule

The following table correlates the monthly income of the respondents and the chance to compromise their occupation schedule for participating in the development programs.

Table 7.17: Monthly Income and Compromise the Occupation Schedule

Monthly Income (Rs.)	Compromise the Occupation Schedule				χ^2	df	p-value
	Always (%)	Some times (%)	Never (%)	Total			
501-1000	4 (2.5)	118 (74.7)	36 (22.8)	158			
1001-3000	7 (6.6)	61 (57.5)	38 (13.8)	106	98.379**	4	0.005
3001-above	20 (55.6)	11 (30.6)	5 (13.9)	36			
Total	31 (10.3)	190 (63.3)	79 (26.3)	300			

** Significant at 1% level ($p < 0.01$)

Table 7.17 presents the monthly income level of the sample respondents in relation to their possibility to compromise their occupation schedule. The informants who earn their monthly income above Rs.3000 had better chance to compromise their working schedule for participating in the developmental activities in the NHGs, SHGs and Gramasabha. These respondents earn their living from poultry, livestock, etc. and can spare their time to improve the self-help groups in the locality. But many of the respondents who had their monthly income below Rs. 3000 could not compromise their schedule for many reasons.

The χ^2 value calculated at 4 degrees of freedom is 98.379 and its p-value is 0.005. Therefore by disposing the null value, it can be concluded that the relationship between monthly income of the respondents and the chance to compromise their occupational schedule to participate in the developmental programmes more significant.

Factors that Block Effective Participation

Women in rural societies are often treated as inferior. Even women accept the dogma that being women, they should lead their lives very differently and subordinate themselves to male wishes. This makes women insecure, lacking a sense of self-worth, and are thus incapable of assuming decisive control over their milieu- social or political. Women are portrayed as submissive. They are not meant to be active and outspoken, particularly in the presence of men or elders. A woman is always questioned in the name of traditional socio-cultural norms that do not allow her to speak out, go alone, talk before elders and take independent decisions. Another factor that blocks her participation is low level of awareness. 115 (38.3%) among the 300 respondents didn't have enough time to participate in the programs,

63 respondents (21%) had lack of confidence,71 respondents (23.7%) suffered from economic constraints, and 51 respondents (17%) were not participating because of their SC identity.

Age and Factors that Block Effective Participation

The factors that prevent effective participation of women is correlated against their age and is presented in the following table.

Table 7.18: Age and factors that block the effective participation

Age	Factors that Block the Respondents					χ^2	df	p-value
	Lack of Time (%)	Lack of Confidence (%)	Economic Constraints (%)	SC Women Identities (%)	Total			
18-25	26 (53.1)	7 (14.3)	10 (20.4)	6 (12.2)	49	17.801*	9	0.038
26-33	41 (44.1)	17 (18.3)	23 (24.7)	12 (12.9)	93			
34-41	27 (32.9)	24 (29.3)	19 (23.2)	12 (14.6)	82			
42 Above	21 (27.6)	15 (19.7)	19 (25)	21(27.6)	76			
Total	115 (38.3)	63 (21)	71 (23.7)	51 (17)	300			

* Significant at 5% level ($p < 0.05$)

The above table very clearly demonstrates the situation which they face in their daily lives. The grass root level women do not have self-confidence, face economic constraints, and their identity itself troubles them. It is evident from the table that 53.1 per cent of the youngsters had not enough time to spend in these programmes, they are not confident as well. Economically they are weak and their identity also stops them. The respondents in age groups of above 42 years faced the problem of their identity. These women have many problems in their personal lives. They have spinster daughters to marry, ailing husbands, and more. In rural societies that are traditional in nature, politics is considered unwomanly (Rajiv and Yasin 2007).

The χ^2 calculated for 9 degrees of freedom is 17.801 and its p-value is 0.038. Therefore by disposing the null value, it can be stated that the factors that block the SC women's effective participation in the programmes has significant correlation with their age.

Education and Factors that Block the Effective Participation

Education is likely to enhance women's economic independence by equipping them with skills necessary for paid employment opportunities, thereby making their economic contribution more visible. Education has the potential of empowering women in different ways, viz. giving confidence, maintain economy, overcome any type of constraints. The table below represents the educational level of the respondents and the factors which block them from participating in the programs.

Table 7.19: Education and factors that block the effective participation

Education	Factors that Block the Respondents					χ^2	df	p-value
	Lack of Time (%)	Lack of Confidence (%)	Economic Constraints (%)	SC women Identities (%)	Total			
Illiterate	11 (19.6)	14 (25)	15 (26.8)	16 (28.6)	56	40.786*	9	0.005
Primary	65 (36.3)	43 (24)	51 (28.5)	20 (11.2)	179			
Pre-degree	24 (54.5)	6 (13.6)	5 (11.4)	9 (20.5)	44			
Graduate	15 (71.4)	–	–	6 (28.6)	21			
Total	115 (38.3)	63 (21)	71 (23.7)	51 (17)	300			

* Significant at 1% level ($p < 0.01$)

The table 7.19 highlights the problems which block SC women from participating in the programmes like SHGs, NHGs. Education has become a necessity in this world just like food and shelter. The education can lift persons from the earth to sky. In this growing world the illiterate people suffer a lot. The above table reflects this reality. Most of the graduate respondents (71.4%) had confidence, they don't have economic constraints, and the only problem they faced was their caste identity (28.6 %). Even though the people are educated, their minds are preoccupied with caste prejudices. Caste identity, irrespective of their educational achievements is a major block in the empowerment of SC women.

The illiterates also find enough time to spend, but they lack confidence, and face economic constraints. They are scared to do even a simple work. The other major factor is caste identity.

The χ^2 calculated for 9 degrees of freedom is 40.786 and its p-value is 0.005, thereby disposing the null value, we derive at that education and the factors that block SC women's effective participation in the programmes is more significantly related.

Age at Marriage and Factors that Block Effective Participation

Early marriage is likely to have negative effect on empowerment by virtually terminating women's access to the sources of empowerment such as formal education (Mason, 1987), awareness, confidence and all needed variables. Table 7.20 presents the factors that affect the respondents' effective participation in relation with their age at marriage.

Table 7.20 examines the problems encountered by the respondents, which block their effective participation. Generally, women in the male dominated society cannot take any decision of their own. They have to depend on men for everything. The women below 18 years, who are unmarried, didn't get time to spend because they are busy with schools and colleges. These young ladies lack confidence than the others. They are not much suppressed with economic constraints; rather they are discriminated on the basis of their caste identity (38.3%).

Table 7.20: Age at marriage and factors that block the effective participation

Age at Marriage	Factors that Block the Respondents					χ^2	df	p-value
	Lack of Time (%)	Lack of Confidence (%)	Economic Constraints (%)	SC Women Identities (%)	Total			
Below 18	13 (27.7)	11 (23.4)	5 (10.6)	18 (38.3)	47	25.600**	6	0.005
18-21	46 (35.4)	28 (21.5)	39 (30)	17 (13.1)	130			
22 above	52 (46.8)	22 (19.8)	24 (21.6)	13 (11.7)	111			
Total	111 (38.5)	61 (21.2)	68 (23.6)	48 (16.7)	288			

** Significant at 1% level ($p < 0.01$)

The 18-22 age group women, when they got married they completely depend on their husbands, in- laws and others. So they could not find time to do anything. They also lack confidence and are the economically deprived. They have to find some occupation for their living. Their caste identities throw them back not allowing them to come up in their life.

The χ^2 value at 6 degrees of freedom is 25.600 and its p-value is 0.005. Thereby disposing the null value, it can be concluded that age at marriage is significantly related to the factors that block SC women's effective participation in the programmes.

Occupation and Factors that Block Effective Participation

Household work is the responsibility of the women, while the public and the political sphere were men's prerogative. Women who did not follow this tradition were seen with disregard. Table 7.21 shows how occupations of the respondents affect their effective participation in group activities.

Table 7.21: Occupation and factors that block the effective participation

Occupation	Factors that Block the Respondents				Total	χ^2	df	p-value
	Lack of Time (%)	Lack of Confidence (%)	Economic Constraints (%)	SC women Identities (%)				
Employed	28 (51.9)	6 (11.1)	9 (16.7)	11 (20.4)	54	32.123**	9	0.005
Self employed	26 (56.5)	8 (17.4)	6 (13)	6 (13)	46			
Labour	38 (30.6)	37 (29.8)	36 (29)	13 (10)5	124			
Unemployed	23 (30.3)	12 (15.8)	20 (26.)	21 (27)	76			
Total	115 (38.3)	63 (21)	71 (23.7)	51 (17)	300			

** Significant at 1% level ($p < 0.01$)

The table above clearly shows that, the respondents from any type of family background face almost the same types of problems in their lives, which blocked them from participating in the programmes in their locality.

They face lack of time and confidence because they are scared. They fear that, if some problem happens it may result in great trouble, and as they are not economically sound they may not be able to solve these problems. But the major problem they face is the bias of higher authorities towards them.

The χ^2 calculated for 9 degrees of freedom is 32.123 and its p-value is 0.005 and by disposing the null value, it is concluded that relation between SC women's occupation types and the factors that block their effective participation in the programmes is more significant.

Monthly Income and Factors that Block Effective Participation

The respondents earn very low income. The correlation between income and factors that block SC women from participating in the SHGs and NHGs is presented in the table.

Table 7.22: Monthly income and factors that block the effective participation

Monthly Income (Rs.)	Factors that block the respondents					χ^2	df	p-value
	Lack of Time (%)	Lack of Confidence (%)	Economic Constraints (%)	SC women Identities (%)	Total			
501-1000	51 (32.3)	46 (29.1)	40 (25.3)	21 (13.3)	158	41.703**	6	0.005
1001-3000	36 (34)	14 (13.2)	31 (29.2)	25 (23.6)	106			
3001-above	28 (77.7)	3 (8.3)	–	5 (13.9)	36			
Total	115(38.3)	63 (21)	71 (23.7)	51 (17.5)	300			

** Significant at 1% level ($p < 0.01$)

The table points the problems SC women belonging to different income categories face which block them from participating in the government's supportive agency meetings. All the four categories have time to spend in these meetings and in its developmental group activities. The problem they face is lack of confidence. The labourers face it more because they lack education. The labourers and the unemployed categories face the problem of economic constraints. The employed and self-employed face the problem of caste identities, the unemployed and the employed face it more severely. The employed respondents face the hindrance from their employed counterparts of other communities, who suppress their views and ideas and trouble them with much insult. The high caste people insult the unemployed SC women by pointing out their caste and unemployment status.

The χ^2 calculated at 6 degrees of freedom is 41.703 and its p-value is 0.005. Hence by rejecting the null value, it is concluded that the monthly income and factors that block their effective participation in the programmes is more significantly related.

Conclusion

The multiplicity of factors that hinder the march of SC women's towards empowerment were analysed in this chapter. Among them, their caste identity was found to be the most significant one. About half of the respondents (48.3 %) said that their caste identity hindered them to some extent from participating in the developmental programmes. 29.7 per cent never felt it as a hindering factor. Further analysis revealed that there was a statistically significant association between hindrance and the variables such as age, education, family type, occupation and income. Among the respondents a significant per cent of the elderly, illiterates, joint family respondents, employees and high income earnings have always been hindered in their participation in SHGs, NHGs and Gramasabhas because of their caste identity. They are often subjected to the teasing by the elites and constrained by lack of awareness, time, employment etc.

Availability of time was found to be another hindering factor. Over half of the respondents (58%) said that non-availability of time acted as a hindrance to some extent and for 29.3 per cent it became a hindrance always. Further analysis revealed that education, occupation and income were statistically significant variables that determine the extent of hindrance imposed on SC women. A comparatively higher per cent of graduates, employed and high income categories among the respondents experienced this problem severely.

Restrictions imposed by the family were another factor analyzed. For 41.7 per cent of the respondents, sometimes it operated as a constraint and for a little over half of them (50.7 %), it never became a constraint. Further analysis showed that age, education, family type, occupation and income were the important intervening variables having statistically proven associations with the dependant variable family restriction. Among the intervening variables; family imposed more restrictions on the elderly, the illiterates, the unemployed and the lower income earning members. The SC women face lots of humiliation on behalf of her caste and sex within their families and outside which pull them back from social involvements.

The need to compromise with the occupation schedule was another significant variable. About two third of the respondents (63.3%) were encouraged to compromise their work schedule to some extent for participating in the developmental programmes of the government. Further analysis showed that the variables such as education, family type, occupation and monthly income had a statistically significant association with the SC women's possibility of compromising their occupational schedules. Among these intervening variables, it was found that a greater constraint on compromising work schedule was imposed on the illiterate, the self-employed and lower income groups.

Among other personal factors that hinder the effective participation in group activities were non-availability of time, economic factors, lack of confidence and caste identity. Further analysis revealed that the independent variables such as age, education, age at marriage, occupation and monthly income have statistically significant association with various constraining factors that block the effective participation of SC women in group activities.

However, it should be borne in mind that effective participation cannot be legalized. It is also useful to remember that engendering of state institutions does not invariably translate into gender equitable policies. It necessitates the creation of an enabling political, social and cultural environment conducive for women to acquire awareness, capabilities and education, to articulate their concerns, and an institutional environment that is receptive and responsive to such concerns. As such, participation is a more broad-based process which encompasses state-society interplay.

8

Summary of Findings and Conclusion

Decentralisation process will empower women only if it becomes an explicit goal, combined with well-defined strategies, adequate resources and commitment at top levels. Panchayat Raj institutions that envisage planning and execution of development activities at local level are a big step towards this end. In Kerala, the democratic decentralisation involves cross-sections of the people, including women in the process of decision-making and development. Democratic decentralisation implies mass participation in local socio-political and economic affairs that affect the ordinary people particularly the scheduled caste women which provides a base for their socio-political and economic sustainability. The supportive systems such as Gramasabhas, Self Help Groups (SHGs) and Neighbourhood Groups (NHGs) provide a platform for the SC women to come to the mainstream and thus empower themselves. But in spite of such formal institutional structures and constitutional provisions, women's social participation and empowerment are not up to the marks. The condition of SC women is more vulnerable thanks to their place at the lower strata of the socio-economic hierarchy. In this context the present study tried to analyse the empowerment of SC women in Kerala through democratic decentralisation. The following objectives were set for the study.

1. To study the specific and general schemes in the democratic decentralisation process for the empowerment of SC women.
2. To examine the implementation of various schemes intended for the empowerment of SC women at various stages of democratic decentralisation.
3. To examine the awareness level of SC women about the various schemes in democratic decentralisation process for the empowerment of SC women.
4. To study the social empowerment of SC women.
5. To analyse the political and economic empowerment of the SC women after the implementation of democratic decentralisation.

6. To study the factors which hinder the empowerment of SC women in the democratic decentralisation process.

The following hypotheses were framed for the study.

1. A considerable size of SC women is not aware of the various schemes.
2. Decentralisation process did not lead to the social empowerment of SC women.
3. Decentralisation process has paved the way for the political and economic empowerment of SC women.
4. There are many constraints which hinder the empowerment of the SC women in the democratic decentralisation process.

Data for the study was collected from a sample of 300 SC women from Palakkad and Thriruvananthapuram districts in Kerala. The sample women were selected through the multistage random sampling and purposive sampling methods. Multistage sampling (four stages) was adopted for the selection of wards. After selecting the districts on the basis of their highest share of SC population,ten panchayats from each district with highest percentage of SC population were identified. From each selected Panchayat, one ward having the highest percentage of SCs has been identified. From each ward, 15 SC households were selected using the purposive sampling method. Purposive sampling method was used for the sample selection as the researcher wanted purposefully select those households having women participating in SHGs, NHGsandGramasabha. One woman from each household who was actively participating in the empowerment programmes was interviewed to collect data for the study.

The study is structured into seven chapters. The first chapter introduces the problem and outlines the review of relevant literature; the methodology is discussed in the second chapter and data analysis is presented inchapters 3-7.

The third chaptercritically analysed the specific and general schemes involved in the democratic decentralisation process along with their implementation at various levels for the empowerment of SC women. This chapter has three parts.

1. Constitutional safeguards;
2. Welfare activities for the development of SC women; and
3. Specific programmes which are in implementation level.

In order to fulfil the promises of the Directive Principles, certain Amendments were made to the Constitution to uplift the SCs and STsfrom their marginalized plight. Moreover the Constitution has special Articles for the welfare of the SCs. Our Constitution follows the policy of protective discrimination. The Article 46 is envisaged toprotect them from social injustice and all forms of exploitation by providing an enabling environment for the welfare of the marginalised groups in the country.

Articles 14, 15 and 16 attempts to ensure equal treatment to every citizen in privileges conferred and liabilities imposed i.e. there should not be favouritism or discrimination. Likewise, there are Articles that require the appointment of ministers from SCs/STs. Articles, 330, 332 and 334 provide for the reservation of seats for SCs/STs in the state Legislatures and Parliament.The Harijan welfare minister is the chief executive for the welfare of the SCs and STs at political and administrative levels. He is assisted by a Secretary of IAS cadre, along with various secretaries and staffs who constitute the secretariat wing. A district level administrative office works for the welfare of the backward and weaker sections. The office is equipped with well-organised structures and men with sympathy for understanding the problems of people.

To develop the SC community, many departments such as Scheduled Caste Development Department were organized by administrative agencies for formulation, implementation, execution and administration of various schemes for the removal of social exclusion and economic backwardness of the SCs in the state.

There are two welfare committees that are set up to look after the welfare of the SCs and STs - the State Welfare Advisory Committee and the Committee for the Removal of Untouchability. The SWAC includes all Scheduled Caste MLAs and meet once in three months to discuss the activities. The DAC will meet as and when required to discuss and tender advice relating to location, allotment of houses, selection of beneficiaries and selection of persons for payment of grants.

Certain welfare activities, the programmes under SCDD, are carried out by KIRTADS and KSDC for SCs and STs; KSBCDC and KSDC for Christian converts from SCs and other recommended communities. They cover wide areas such as education, health and housing which promote the economic and social welfare of SCs and Other Backward Classes.

Special Central Assistance, though not linked with any programme or scheme, supplements the efforts of the state for the economic development of the SCs. The welfare schemes were implemented through the Special Component Plan. After its implementation, monitoring and evaluation were carried out and periodic progress reports were submitted to the Central Government by the respective state governments. In spite of all these efforts, in reality, funds are not properly utilised and every year it gets lapsed. Follow up programmes are also often defective. Thus, even though many programmes exist for the uplift of the weaker sections, they are neither utilised properly nor do they reach the hands of the deserving parties. Proper steps need to be taken in this regard by the government and other concerned departments.

Chapter four deals with the awareness level and the empowerment of SC women. This chapter examines the awareness level of SC women about the various schemes in democratic decentralisation process that are implemented for the empowerment of SC women based on certain indicators. The first indicator was awareness and analysis based on this indicator revealed that majority of the respondents was aware of the welfare schemes through varied sources to some extent. It was found that educated respondents were more aware about the functions of the government agencies. This reveals that the relationship between educational attainment and awareness were quite significant. The data was further analysed to find the relationship between age at marriage and awareness about the functions of government agencies and it was found that the respondents who married after the age of 22 years were more aware about the functions of government agencies. It was further found that the respondents who earned a monthly income of Rs. 3000/- and above were more aware of the functions of the government agencies.

The second indicator was the knowledge of specific programmes of government agencies. The data revealed that higher level of awareness was found among the graduates, self-employed and the higher income categories. It was also identified that respondents with little education did not get any support from other agencies. The graduates, employed and high income groups availed more support from the agencies such as JSS, STED and NGOs.With respect to the indicator, right to speak in the public meetings, 78.7 per cent of the respondents were aware of their right to speak in the public meetings. Of the remaining,73.7 per cent were hesitantto speak in the public meetings due to shyness. This indicates that mere awareness does not transform the social conditions of SC women. More concerted efforts are needed to change the patriarchal mind set of the communities.

Participation in the developmental agencies was another indicator against which data was collected and analysed. Generally, the participation in various programmes is expected togenerate more awareness. But in the study, only less than a quarter of the respondents benefited in such a way. Education, family type and occupation had a significant role in the process. Utilization of resources was another indicator analysed. The analysis showed that age, family type and the monthly income had statistically significant association with the utilization of resources. The analysis further revealed that most of the respondents were aware of the programmes only to some extent. These findings supported the first hypothesis: aconsiderable size of the SC women was not aware of the various schemes. Most of the elderly, hailing from joint families, illiterates, the respondents with age at marriage of 18-21 years, the monthly income earners of Rs. 501-1000 and the labourer categories of respondents were not aware of various schemes.

However, the better placed segments within the excluded 'SC women' category were more aware of the developmental initiates. Thus it is imperative to sensitise the policy makers about such issues and effective implementation system to be gauged for taking up any new development initiatives that would support the most weaker sections among SC women.

Chapter five deals with the empowerment of SC women. Indicators such as decision-making, travelling without male escorts and participation in social service activities are analysed as chief components of the empowerment of SC women. It was found that 54 per cent of the respondents rarely took part in the decision making process within their families and participation in the programmes of the government agencies gave the confidence to involve in the decision making process for 33.7 per cent of the respondents. For almost half of the respondents, the involvement in decision making process increased to some extent after attending the government programmes. This points to the necessity of social exposure of SC women in their empowerment process. Further analysis reveals that the level of involvement in the decision making process is relatively higher among the younger age categories of SC women.

With respect to the preference for male child, it was found that over 3/4th of the respondents (78%) did not show any preference for male children and this trend was more predominant among the highly educated and high income categories among the respondents. Analysis of data on the freedom of mobility has shown that the participation in the SHGs, NHGs and Gramasabhas have shown significant improvement in their freedom of mobility irrespective of their level of education.

The findings on the empowerment of SC women support the hypothesis that SC women experienced low levels of social empowerment. The overall picture of the empowerment of SC women reveals that their level of social sensitivity and social responsibility got improvised as a result of the involvement with the developmental initiatives implemented through the PRI system. As a whole, this chapter brings out the importance of SC women's participation in the decision making process in order to ensure their empowerment.

The sixth chapter adheres to the economic empowerment of SC women. Economic empowerment is measured against the variables such as change in income levels, status of family, saving habits, control over income, power to dispose of assets and money lending. Data on income levels was analysed against the variables such as age, education and monthly income of the respondents and was found that, in general, for majority of the respondents income levels increased only to some extent. It has been found that income level of the respondents increased fairly with their age. 31.3 per cent of the respondents have improved their habit of saving as a result of their association with the government programmes. For 50 per cent of the respondents, their savings remained the same.

With respect to control over income, it was found that 49.7 per cent of the respondents had control over their income to some extent. It was further identified that higher level of control over income was exercised by the respondents belonging to the younger age, educated, nuclear family, employed and lower and higher income categories.It was also found that age and educational attainment of the respondents have a direct bearing on the capacity to dispose assets. Majority of the respondents who could use their assets belonged to the younger age, with higher education and nuclear family respondents. Analysis of the money lending habit of the respondents revealed a mixed result. Over half of the respondents (51.7%) still approached the money lenders for availing loans. The dependency of SC women on money lenders gives us a warning that economic wellbeing alone is not the sufficient condition to keep the SC women away from the clutches of the money lenders. Conscious efforts need to be taken in this regard.

The above analysis revealed that decentralisation process helped in the economic empowerment of SC women and thus proves a part of the third hypothesis, namely, decentralisation process has paved the way for the economic empowerment of SC women.

The last chapter presents the major constraints experienced by SC women. The situation of SC women is pathetic as they are constrained by caste barriers, education, income, asset ownership and low status. They need special assistance to come out of these constraints. Participation in SHGs, NHGs and Gramasabhas is a way out in this process. In the present study the factors hindering empowerment are assessed against the independent variables such as age, education, family type and occupation. The first indicator considered here is the caste identity which has a direct bearing on the individual, familial and social spheres of SC women's life. SC women are educationally and economically backward than others which force them to remain isolated from the mainstream. They are forced to undergo various kinds of discriminations which adversely affect their confidence level. Around half of the respondents (48.3%) expressed the feeling of being discriminated and humiliated by the upper castes. 22 per cent expressed their feeling that their caste identity actually hinders their participation in various government programmes.

In several families SC women are sole bread winners. Circumstances force them to take care of their children and parents. This in fact adds to their burden. They rarely find free time so that they could engage in the activities of SHGs, NSGs and Gramasabhas. This actually stands in the way of their empowerment.

Family restriction is another factor that prevent SC women's social participation. SC women are often ill-treated, hurt and humiliated by others in the society including by the members of their own family. The present study revealed that restrictions within the family were highly experienced by the elderly, illiterate, unemployed and low income categories.

The heavy workload of SC women often forces them to compromise their occupation schedule. It was found that 66.3 per cent of the respondents were some way or other forced to compromise their occupation schedule to some extent. As in the above cases this constraint was also experienced mostly by the illiterate, self-employed and lower income groups. The findings of the study in this regard proves that irrespective of the numerous claims by the social scientists about the Kerala model of development, the family rooted age old 'caste discrimination' coupled with the practice of 'patriarchy' constrain the empowerment process of SC women.

Several factors have been identifies as blocking the effective participation of SC women in the SHGs, NHGs and Gramasabhas. Significant among them are time, economic factors, lack of confidence, caste identity and family restrictions. The independent variables such as age, education, age at marriage, occupation and monthly income have significant association with the constraining factors that block the effective participation of SC women in group activities. These factors actually hinder the effectiveness of the decentralisation process in the case of SC women. Thus the fourth hypothesis, 'the existing governmental mechanisms are not enough to empower the SC women', is proved here.

Rowlands pointed out that empowerment process will take a form which arises out of a particular economic, geographic, political and social location; out of specific life experience and out of the interaction of the above with the gender relations prevailing in that society. In the present study, the empowerment of SC women has been motivated by the specific life experience as a result of their participation in Gramasabha and other such political bodies. Women organized to promote their self-reliance, assert their independent rights, make choices and control resource will assist in challenging and eliminating their age old subordination. Thus empowerment in the participatory process ranging from home to community which later may lead to self-reliance as put forth by Keller and Mbew stands proved in the case of SC women.

The SC women through participating in the meetings of groups and involvement in the group activities have gained 'power with' through savings and loans, better economic conditions and control over wages earned by them; had 'power to', through awareness and knowledge, decision making and mobility; and exercised 'power over' their resources. Here the power theory of Rowlands is well accepted.

Thus there has been a transition of the SC women from the state of powerlessness to a state of relative control over one's life, destiny and environment.

The study supports Amartya Sen's theory of development of freedom. It was found that low participation of SC women in the day to day activities of SHGs and NHGs were due to their lack of accesses. The participation of women in SHGs and NHGs leads not merely to the generation of income but also to the enhancement of the status and increased independence.

Suggestions

1. The SC women should be made to realize the importance of specific programmes undertaken by the agencies like NGOs, JSS and STED
2. The SC women should be motivated to organize themselves for achieving their social and economic empowerment.
3. Training and awareness programmes should be suitably modified to make them more effective and meaningful for the empowerment of SC women.
4. Specialized agencies should be entertained for promoting the empowerment of SC women and for the effective utilization of the increased awareness SC women.
5. The SC women who are not the members of SHGs/NHGs should be motivated to organize themselvesso as to liberate themselves from the male domination.
6. The local bodies such as Grama Panchayats and Block Panchayats should be encouraged to have regular interactions with the SC women for their empowerment. The government should also support the Panchayat authorities through direct contact.
7. Educational and political awareness in all age groups should be promoted among the SC women.
8. The lending institutions, policies and regulations should be made more liberal and accessible to SC women for enabling them to break the economic barriers in the way of their empowerment.

Bibliography

BOOKS

Abbasayulu, Y.B. 1978. A Social Study of the Scheduled Caste Legislators of Andhra Pradesh Hyderabad. Book Links Co-operation.

Anuradha, Sharma. 1998. Encyclopedia of Indian Women. Vol. III. New Delhi: Commonwealth Publishers.

Baily, F.G. 1971. Caste and Economic Frontier. Bombay: Oxford University Press.

Basu, A. 2003. Gender and Governance: Concepts and Contexts in Essays on Gender and Governance. India: UNDP.

Batliwala, S. 1995. The meaning of Women's Empowerment: New Concepts from Action. In G. Sen, A. Germain, and L.C. Chen (eds.), Population Policies Reconsidered: Health, Empowerment, and Rights. Boston: Harvard University Press.

Bernad, S. 1955. The Changing Status of a Depressed Caste, Village India, (ed) by Mackim Marriot. Bombay: Asia Publishing House.

Bhandari. 2009. Role and Status of Women in New Panchayati Raj System - Decentralization and Rural Development. New Delhi: Alfa Publications.

Bhattacharya, M. 2002. Panchayat Raj in West Bengal. Democratic Decentralization or Democratic Centralism. New Delhi: Manak Publication Pvt, Ltd.

Biju, M.R (2009). Democratic Political Process, Mittal Publications New Delhi.

Braye, S. and Preston M. Shoot. 1995. Empowering Practice in Social Case Work. Buckingham: Open University Press.

Chalam, K.S. 2008. Modernization and Dalit Education. New Delhi: Rawat Publication.

Chatterjee, S.K. (ed), 1996. The Scheduled Castes in India. Vol. IV. New Delhi: Gyan Publishing House.

Chatterjee, S.K. 2008. The Scheduled Castes in India. Jaipur: Gyan Publishing House.

Chitkara, M.G. 2001. Women and Social Transformation. New Delhi: A.P.H Publishing Corporation.

Chudhuri, N.C. 1978. Womanhood in Tribal India. Calcutta: Indian Anthropological Society.

Dubey, S.N. 1973. Administration of Social Welfare Programmes in India. Bombay: Somaiya Publications Pvt. Ltd.

Dubey. 1971. Social Policy in Conditions of Dynamic Change, Bombay.

Eber, C.E. and Rosenbaum, B. 1993. That we may serve Beneath your Hands and Feet: Women Weavers in Highland Chiapas, Mexico. In J. Nash (ed). Crafts in the World Market: The Impact of Global Exchange on Middle American Artisans: Albany State University of New York Press.

Friedmann, J. 1992. Empowerment: The Politics of Alternative Development, Cambridge: Blackwell.

Ghosh. G. 1997. Dalit Women. New Delhi: APH. Publishing Corporation.

Harold, I. 1965. India's Ex-untouchables. Bombay: Asian Publishing House.

Inkels, A. 1976. The Modernization of Man in Socialist and Non-socialists Countries, in Mark, G Field (ed.), Social Consequences of Modernization in Communist Countries . John Hopkins. Baltimore: University Press.

Isaac, T.M. and R.W. Franke. 2000. Local Democracy and Development. People's Campaign for Decentralized Planning in Kerala. New Delhi: Left World Books.

Joshi, B. 1960. Democracy in Search of Equality: Untouchable Politics and Indian Social Change. Delhi: Hindustan Publication.

Kabeer, N. 1994. Reversed Realities: Gender Hierarchies in Development thought. London: New York.

Kabeer, N. 2001. Reflections on the Measurement of Women's Empowerment: In Discussing Women's Empowerment-Theory and Practice. Stockholm: Novum Grafiska AB.

Karpagam, and Jaya. Arunachalam. 2008. Rural Women and Development in India: Issues and Challenges. New Delhi: Rawat Publications.

Klugman, J. 2002. A Sourcebook for Poverty Reduction Strategies. Vol. 1 Core Techniques and Crosscutting Issues. Washington: The World Bank.

Lakshminarayana, H.D. 1980. Democracy in Rural India. New Delhi: National Publishing House.

Lekshmana, C. 1977. Harijinas and the Social Discrimination. A Study of some Telangana Village. Hydrabad.

Lele, Uma. 1975 The Design of Rural Development: Lessons from Africa. John Hopkins University Press

Manick Yamba. 1989. Women in Panchayat Raj Structures. New Delhi: Gyan Publishing House.

Mathew, K.K. 2003. Impact of Welfare Programmes on the Life of SCs in Kerala: A Case Study of the Pulayas, PhD Thesis.

Mehtra, G.S. 2008. Participation of Women in the Panchayati Raj System. New Delhi: Kanishka Publishers.

Mendelson, O and Vicziamy. 1998. The Untouchables. Cambridge University Press.

Modi, S.K. 2008. Socio-Economic Development of Dalits in India. New Delhi: Navyug Publishers and Distributors.

Murty, S. 2008. Socio-Economic Status and Awareness of Scheduled Caste Women. New Delhi: RBSA Publishers.

Narasimhan, S. 1999. Empowering Women: An Alternative Strategy from Rural India. New Delhi: Sage Publications.

Parvathamma, C. 1989, Scheduled Castes at the Cross Roads. New Delhi: Ashish Publishing House.

Patwardhan, Sunanda. 1973. Change among the India's Harijians, Maharastra: A Case Study. New Delhi: Orient Longman Ltd.

Purushothaman, S. 1998. The Empowerment of Women in India: Grassroots Women's Networks and the State. New Delhi: Sage Publications.

Putnam, R.D. and R. Leonardi and R. Nanetti. 1993. Making Democracy Work Civic Traditions in Modern Italy.

Rahman, A. 1999. Women and Microcredit in Rural Bangladesh, Anthropological Study of the Rhetoric and Realities of Grameen Bank Lending. Boulder USA: West view Press.

Ramashray, Roy. 1999. Dalits Development and Democracy, New Delhi: Shipra Publication.

Ramashray, Roy. and B. Sing. 1987. Between Two Worlds. A Study of Harijan Elites. New Delhi: Discovery Publishing House.

Reddy, 2002. Empowering Communities through Participatory methods. New Delhi: Manak Publications.

Rowlands, Joanna. 1997. Question Empowerment. Oxford: Oxfam Publications.

Santhakumari, R. 1982. The Scheduled Caste and Welfare Measures. New Delhi: Classical Publishing House.

Schidananda. 1977. The Harijan Elite. Delhi: Thomas Press.

Shymlal, 1984. The Bangi in Transition. New Delhi: Inter India Publications.

Singh. D. K. 2001. Surplus Land Distribution and Its Impact on Socio-economic Status of Scheduled Castes in U.P: Poorvanchal Manav Kalyan Sansthan, Mahrajganj.

Soran, Singh. 1987. Scheduled Caste of India Dimensions of Social Change. New Delhi: Gian Publishing House.

Soundari, M.H and M.A. Sudhir. 2001. Self-help Groups for Sustainable Rural Development in S.P, Jain *(ed)* Emerging Institutions for Decentralised Rural Development, Vol. II. Hydrabad: NIRD.

Subramanyam, P. 2003. Rural Development Policies and Some Innovative Projects in Asia and The Pacific: An Overview in Dynamics of Sustainable Rural Development by (ed) Reddy and Subramanyam. New Delhi: Serials Publications. Sudrastan Books.

Sunderaj, Victor. 1994. Predictors of Social Mobility. Profile of the Innovative and Non-Innovative SCs of Rural Tamil Nadu, Temple University. Ph.D. Thesis.

Sunderaj, Victor. 1994. SC of Rural India: Problems and Prospects, New Delhi: APH Publishing.

Thind, G. 1999. Our Indian Subcontinent Heritage. British Colombia: Cross Town Press Ltd.

Vakil A.K. (ed). 1985. Reservation Policy and SCs in India. New Delhi: APH Publishers.

Vidya, K.C. 1997. Political Empowerment of Women at the Grassroots New Delhi: Kanishka Publishers.

JOURNALS

Agarwal, Deepti, 2001. Empowerment of Rural Women in India, Social Welfare, Vol. 48, No. 4, July.

Annapurna, Nautiyal, 2003. Women and Development in the Garhwal Himalyas, AJWS Vol. 9, No. 4.

Aparna Mitra, 2008. The Status of Women among the Scheduled Tribes in India. The Journal of Socio-Economics 37.

Archana, Sinha and Shalu Nigam, Time to Change Track? Social Welfare, Vol. 47, No. 5, August 2000.

Archana, Patkar, Socio-Economic Status and Female Literacy in India, Int, J. Educational Development.Vol. 15, No. 4, 1995.

Batliwala, Srilatha. 1994. "The meaning of Women's Empowerment: New Concepts from Action." pp. 127-138 in Population Policies Reconsidered: Health, Empowerment and Rights. G. Sen, A. Germain, and L.C. Chen, eds. Cambridge, MA: Harvard University Press.

Chauhan, S.K, 1976. Social Mobility in Upper Assam, in Social Action.

Dwarakanth, H.D. 2003, Saving and Credit Movement in Andhra Pradesh: Participation of Rural Women, Kurukshetra, Vol. 51, No. 4.

Gupta K.N. 2001, Women's Empowerment and Protection of their Rights, Social Welfare, Vol. 47, No. 12, March.

Gurumoorthy, T.R, Self-help Groups Empower Rural Women, Kurukshetra, Feb., 2000.

James Antony. M., Role of Education in Empowering Women, Kerala Sociologist Journal of the Kerala Sociological Society, Vol. 32. No. 1, June 2004.

Lakshmi, Seetha.V, 2004: Womens and Political Empowerment, Kerala Sociologist, Journal of the Kerala Sociological Society, Vol. XXXII. No. 1, June.

Lee, J.A. 1997. Social Movements: Revolution, Reform and Reaction. NACLA's Report on the Americas 30, 13-18.

Malhotra, Anju and Mark Mather, 2003. "Do Schooling and Work Empower Women in Developing Countries? Gender and Domestic Decisions in Sri Lanka." Sociological Forum: 12(4): 599-630.

Mank, D. 1994. The Underachievement of Supported Employment: A call for Reinvestment. Journal of Disability Policy Studies, 5(2).

Mason, Karen Oppenheim, 1987. The Status of Women: Conceptual and Methodological Issues in Demographic Studies, Sociological Forum, 1(2).

Mayoux, L. 2001, 'Women's Empowerment Versus Sustainability? Towards a New Paradigm in Micro-finance Programmes', in Lemire, B, Pearson, R., and Campbell, G. (ed.) Women and Credit; Researching the Past, Refiguring the Future. Berg, Oxford.

Moser, C.O.N. Community Participation in Urban Projects in the Third Word, Progress in Planning, Vol. 32 (2), 1989.

Neel, Mukherjee, 1996, Gender Equality and well being of Rural Women, Yojana, January.

Oldfield, 1990, Citizenship: An Unnatural Pratices; Political quarterly, 61, pp. 177-87.

Palanithurai, G, New Panchayati Raj System in Tamil Nadu, South Asian Journal of Socio-Political Studies, January-June 2001.

Parsons, T. On the Concept of Political Power Proceedings of the American Philosophical Society, 107 (3), 1963.

Puhazhendhi, V. and Satyasai, Economic And Social KJ.S., Empowerment of Rural Poor Through SHG's, Indian Journal of Agricultural Economics, Vol. 56 (3), July-Sept., 2001.

Ramaswamy, U. 1974. Scheduled Castes in Andhra. Some Aspects of Social Change. EPW. Vol. 9, No. 29, pp. 1953-58.

Rao, V.M. Women Self-help Groups: Profiles From Andhra Pradesh and Karnataka, Kurukshetra, April, 2002.

Roy, K.A Chaudhuri, 2008. Influence of Socio-economic Status, Wealth and Financial Empowerment on Gender differences in Health and Healthcare Utilization in later Life: Evidence from India, Journal of Social Science and Medicine.

Satish, P, Some Issues in the Formational of SHG's. Indian Journal of Agricultural Economics, Vol. 56 (3), July-Sept., 2001.

Sinha, A.I. 1996. The State Class and Sena Nexus, EPW, No. 2.

Sooryamoorthy, 2005. Is Kerala Becoming a Knowledge Society?-Evidence from the Scientific Community. Sociological Bulletin, Journal of the Indian Sociological Society, Vol. 53, Number. 2, May-August,

Sticht, T. 1994. Family Literacy: A World movement. Paris, France: UNESCO.

Sticht, T. and McDonald, B. 1990. Teach the Mother and Reach the Child: Literacy Across Generations. Geneva: UNESCO.

Suguna, B, 2001, "Women's Empowerment: Concept and Framework", Social Welfare, Vol. 48, No. 9, December, p. 18.

Supriya G. 2008. The Impact of Lending to Women on Household Vulnerability and Women's Empowerment: Evidence from India, World Development Vol. xx, No. x, pp. xxx-xxx, (Article in Press).

Tripp, R.B. 1981. Farmers and Traders: Some Economic Determinants of Nutritional Status in Northern Ghana. Journal of Tropical Pediatrics, 27, 15-22.

White, D-Leonard. 1959. Implementing Decentralization Programmes in Asia: A Comparative Analysis, Public Administration and Development, 3(3), Washington DC.

Wolfe, Marshall. Participation, The View from Above, UNRISD Dialogue about Participation, No. 3, September, 1983.

WORKING PAPER

Amin, B. 1998. NGO-Promoted Micro Credit Programs and Women's Empowerment in Rural Bangladesh: Quantitative and Qualitative Evidence, The Journal of Developing Areas, Winter,: 221-236.

Bisnath, Savitri and Diane Elson. 1999. Women's Empowerment Revisited. Background Paper, Progress of the World's Women. UNIFEM.

Cain. M. Khonam, S.K. and Nahar. S. 1979. Class, Patriarchy and the Structure of Women's Work in Rural Bangladesh, Centre for Policy Studies Working Papers No. 43. The Population Council of New York.

Eyben, R, 2004. Linking Power and Poverty Reduction in also World Bank Policy Research Working paper.

Grimes, K. 2000. Democratizing International Production and trade: North American Alternative Trade Organizations. In K. Grimes & L. Milgram (Eds.). Artisans and Cooperatives: Developing Alternative Trade for the Global Economy (pp. 11-24). Tucson: University of Arizona Press.

Issac, T.M. 2003. 'Women Elected Representatives in Kerala (1995-2000): From Symbolism to Empowerment', Paper Presented at the Workshop on 'Women's.

Kabeer, N. 1998. 'Money Can't Buy Me Love'? Re-evaluating Gender, Credit and Empowerment in Rural Bangladesh. IDS Discussion Paper 363.

Keller, B. and D.C. Mbwewe. 1991. "Policy and Planning for the Empowerment of Zambia's Women Farmers." Canadian Journal of Development Studies 12(1):75-88 as cited in Rowlands, Jo. 1995. "Empowerment Examined." Development in Practice 5(2): 101-107.

Mac, Mohan. 1961. Participatory Development and Empowerment; the Dangers of Localism, Third World Quarterly, Vol. 21, pp. 247-268.

Malhotra, Anju, Schuler Sidney and Boender Carol. 2002. Measuring Women's Empowerment as a Variable in International Development. Paper Commissioned by the Gender and Development Group of the World Bank, in Support of an ongoing Policy Research Effort on Gender and Development Issues, and by the World Bank's Social Development Group, with Funding from a Norwegian Trust Fund, as Part of a Larger Study on Empowerment and Social Inclusion.

Mencher, J. 1988. Women's Work and Poverty: Women's Contribution to Household Maintenance in South India. In: Dwyer D, Bruce J, eds. A Home Divided: Women and Income in the Third World. Stanford, Calif, USA: Stanford University Press: 99-119.

Mirala, A.V. 1983. The Impact of Women's Employment on Households and Family Life, (Paper Presented in Expert Group Affecting on Form and Looking Strategies for the Advancement of Women, Bangkok.

Puhazhehdhi, V. 1999. Evaluation Study of SHG's: Important Findings of Evaluation Study in Tamil Nadu, Paper Presented in A Workshop, Dated 26-27 August, BIRD, Lucknow.

Radha, S and Bulum, Roy Choudhury. 2002. Women in Local Bodies, Discussion Paper, No. 40, and Thiruvananthapuram: Kerala Research Programme on Local Level Development, Centre for Development Studies.

Salway, S Jesmin, S. and Rahman, S. 2005. Women's Employment in Urban Bangladesh: A Challenge to Gender Identity? Development and Change, 36(2).

Schuler, S. Hashemi, S.M. and Badal, S.H. 'Men's Violence against Women in Rural Bangladesh: Undermined or Exacerbated by Microcredit Programmes?' Development in Practice, Vol. 8, No. 2, May 1998.

Index

❑ ❑ ❑ ❑ ❑